PRAYER

a beginner's guide

Text copyright © Jane Holloway 2000, 2009
The author asserts the moral right
to be identified as the author of this work

Published by
The Bible Reading Fellowship
15 The Chambers, Vineyard
Abingdon OX14 3FE
United Kingdom
Tel: +44 (0)1865 319700
Email: enquiries@brf.org.uk
Website: www.brf.org.uk

ISBN 978 1 84101 611 5
First published 2000 by Hodder & Stoughton Ltd under the title
Prayer for Amateurs

Revised and updated edition published 2009
10 9 8 7 6 5 4 3 2 1 0

Acknowledgments
Unless otherwise stated, scripture quotations are taken from the Holy Bible,
New International Version, copyright © 1973, 1978, 1984 by International
Bible Society, and are used by permission of Hodder & Stoughton Publishers,
a division of Hodder Headline Ltd. All rights reserved. 'NIV' is a registered
trademark of International Bible Society. UK trademark number 1448790.

Scripture quotations from THE MESSAGE. Copyright © by Eugene H. Peterson
1993, 1994, 1995. Used by permission of NavPress Publishing.

A catalogue record for this book is available from the British Library

Printed in Singapore by Craft Print International Ltd

PRAYER

a beginner's guide

Jane Holloway

With grateful thanks to my friends
who have taught me how to pray

Contents

1 Introduction

As you pick up this book, you may not realize it, but you are joining the growing numbers of Christians who are beginning to understand just what an important role prayer has to play in their daily lives. When this book was first published, I worked as the Prayer Co-ordinator with the Evangelical Alliance UK and was in touch with many individuals, churches, organizations and networks that were beginning to pray for different towns and cities and issues across the nation. Today, the numbers and types of prayer initiatives are continuing to grow. I still have the privilege, working with the World Prayer Centre Birmingham as their National Prayer Director, of being in touch with many prayer-based ministries and churches, and with people being drawn to pray around our country. Prayer is definitely on God's agenda.

The growth of round-the-clock, day-and-night or 24-7 praying is on the increase both across Britain and around the world. Thanks to the 24-7 Prayer movement, which was started on the south coast of England in 1999, we have seen a wide range of churches and denominations commit to a year of day-and-night praying. We have also seen hundreds of churches and communities take up the challenge of a 24-7 prayer week, which has led to involvement in local and overseas mission (see http://uk.24-7prayer.com). During the 2007 year of prayer in preparation for Hope08, churches organized 24-7 prayer cover for Manchester and London; in fact, London has continued to maintain this watch of prayer. Citywide 24-7 prayer chains are started by inviting different churches to take a day or a week to engage their congregations in praying for local and national needs.

We have witnessed the rise of special seasons of prayer. Over recent years, Prayer Week has been used by God to unite individuals and churches locally, nationally and globally to pray together for a week in May. Organizations such as the Evangelical Alliance now provide prayer guides through the season of Advent just before Christmas. Churches in the Hull region have taken the lead in providing resources to help churches pray through the season of Lent (before Easter). And the Global Day of Prayer initiative has mobilized prayer all around the world for ten days before Pentecost Sunday. (We will discover more about this in Chapter 4.)

There has been an increase in the way individuals and churches are reconnecting with issues in their communities through prayer: for example, through partnerships with the police, working to reduce crime and the causes of crime. Prayer initiatives are now in place for social justice, education, arts and media, health, education, sport, the family, the environment, economy and government, the workplace and for the mission of the church.

Here in Britain you will find many young people involved in prayer initiatives through a range of organizations and networks. Children are meeting before going to school and hundreds of teenagers connecting via mobile phones and networking websites. There are networks of Christians who link up to pray across the whole of Britain, including in every parliament and assembly building. There are interchurch groups praying in many towns, villages and cities. In the London Docklands, thousands of people gather to pray quarterly through the night for London and Britain as a whole.

A number of ministries have joined together to provide prayer resources: for example, Prayer Alert, Prayer Magazine, Prayer Diary, Pray Right Now and a website to enable people to access these resources and up-to-date news for prayer.[1] As you will discover as you read this book, prayer is no longer something that takes place only inside a church building. God, by his Holy Spirit, is compelling churches to offer prayer for their communities through prayer walking and healing rooms, prayer tents and so on.

Before the year of mission in 2008, Hope08 was launched at a national prayer day ('Trumpet Call') and a year of prayer took place, with Christians uniting on Fridays to pray for their friends and neighbours as well as for national issues. In many of the 1450 communities that took part, regular interchurch prayer meetings were an integral part of their mission.

This increase in prayer is not restricted to the UK. The worldwide movement for prayer was described a number of years ago as 'out of control'—and it still is today! Through the International Prayer Council it is now possible to link up with what is going on in prayer around the world. Christians from different countries have had onsite prayer meetings at almost every G8 meeting since 2000. There was a historic prayer meeting, which I had the privilege of taking part in, at the United Nations building in New York in September 2005. Around 500 Christians (adults and children), from about 45 nations, gathered at the invitation of one of the embassies to spend two days praying for the whole work of the UN and especially for the Millennium Development Goals. We were joined at one session by 25 ambassadors who welcomed the offer of prayer for them in their roles.

Not only is prayer growing but the gospel is spreading faster than it has ever done in history. Throughout the world, more than 100,000 people become Christians every day. Could there be a connection between this and the growth in prayer? I believe that there is.

There were no Christians in Korea 100 years ago. Now, a third of the population of South Korea is vibrantly Christian. What could account for such phenomenal growth? Prayer! Most Christians spend an hour a day from 5 to 6am and the whole of Friday night in prayer, and thousands go to the country's famous Prayer Mountain.

Nepal has witnessed remarkable growth in the Christian church since a group was formed in 1959 with 29 Christians. According to *Operation World*:

By 1985 there were about 50,000 believers. At the climax of persecution in 1990 there were 200,000. By 2000 there were 400,000; some estimate even 500,000 in 3000 or more congregations. The secret: prayer, willingness to suffer for Jesus, dynamic Nepali initiative in evangelism and church planting, and God's miracle-working power.[2]

Other stories of how God has used prayer and unity to bring about remarkable change in communities and nations are being researched, documented and made available through videos and DVDs.[3]

These stories do not tell the whole story, however. Even more remarkable is the fact that many of the people involved in these stories are ordinary church members.

They are not professionals but amateurs in prayer.

- Amateurs who believe that God is powerful and hears and answers prayer.
- Amateurs who know that prayer is not trying to twist God's arm, but is his chosen way of extending his kingdom.
- Amateurs like the couple I met who started praying with other Christians for their neighbours, and now describe it as 'the best thing we have ever done in our lives'.

Prayer is God's gift for all his people. I am certainly an amateur when it comes to prayer. There is much about it that I don't understand and I certainly don't find it easy. But I have discovered that prayer is one of the most exciting and life-changing aspects of being a follower of Jesus Christ.

Prayer lies at the heart of Christianity, and yet most Christians would agree with non-religious people who pray that we all have much to learn about it. Many of us will remember the massive response to the death of Princess Diana, and the shock after 9/11 in New York and 7/7 in London. Millions wanted to pray but had no idea how to go about it.

So in our next chapter we will look at one of the most common questions asked about prayer: what is it?

A prayer

God, I feel pretty hopeless at prayer. Please show me its value and teach me to pray. Amen

2 What is prayer?

Prayer is relationship

Prayer is essentially relationship with God, and it is this relationship that is at the heart of the Christian faith. It is amazing to realize that the God who created all that we see around us in the universe wants you and me to be in regular touch with him.

All relationships have to be worked at in order to survive. What holds people together is love built on friendship, daily contact, honest talking and shared lives. It is the same in our relationship with God. We can think of prayer as a conversation between us and God. He wants us to talk and listen, and to allow our lives to touch his. We can talk to God just as we talk with each other—using words. We can 'talk' with him in silence. Just as we communicate with another person with a look, a smile, a hug or a kiss, we can also learn to relate to God by using our bodies (which we will explore further in Chapter 11).

But if prayer is a conversation with God, and God is Father, Son and Holy Spirit, which part of God are we talking to? And does it matter?

Praying to God as Father

If you find it difficult to grasp the idea of God wanting us to pray, you are not alone. Jesus' disciples took a while to get the idea. As Jews they were used to praying, but as they watched Jesus they realized that they were missing something. As they heard him pray they recognized that Jesus had a very close relationship with God, something that they had not experienced. So they asked him to teach them to pray. Jesus told them that they could come to God in prayer as if he was their father (Matthew 6:9). They were amazed! He said they were to use the word *Abba*, which in their language meant 'Daddy' or 'dear father'. It was the word commonly used by younger children speaking to their earthly fathers.

Prayer is not something we 'say' to a distant God; when we pray, we come as God's children to our Father in heaven. A friend of mine, John, tells this story about one of his grandsons. When Andrew was six years old, he spent a week in the summer staying with his other grandparents on their farm. They loved having him and told him many times just how invaluable he was in helping them. When Andrew went home, he enjoyed telling everyone that his grandparents were having trouble running the farm without him. As John was laughing over this, God nudged him. 'John, you've been like little Andrew with me! You've treated me like a helper in the sky.' John felt God tell him that the image of Andrew going off on the tractor and sitting on his other grandfather's lap was actually a picture of how prayer should be. The moments of greatest delight in God's relationship with us are when we, in childlike dependence and faith, climb on to his lap in prayer, put our hand on his hand and pour out our hearts to him. He is simply waiting for us to get on board.

I remember when, a few years ago, a small group of us met in our church to pray for our vicar, who was going to teach in Nigeria for two weeks. As we prayed, it became very evident that we were praying to our heavenly Father who knew everything about the trip. We all left with a profound sense of peace that he would take care of it all. And God did! Our vicar was kept safe and well and was able to offer some very relevant teaching to the churches he visited.

Praying through Jesus

We pray to our heavenly Father through Jesus, 'for through him we... have access to the Father by one Spirit' (Ephesians 2:18). Jesus taught the disciples that they should pray to the Father in his name (John 14:13–14; 15:16). To pray in his name does not simply mean that we use his name as a formula, but rather that when we do so we confess his name and acknowledge that he is the only way to the Father.

As we pray, we direct our minds and thoughts in faith towards God and then share with him what is on our hearts. Praying is as simple as making a phone call. Before the days of direct dialling, everyone had to find a telephone, ring up an operator and ask to be put through to the number wanted. Today, with mobile phone technology, we can dial anyone, anywhere in the world, wherever we are. Through his death on the cross and his resurrection, Jesus makes it possible for our prayers always to get through to our Father in heaven. We will never get the 'engaged' or 'number unobtainable' tones. We will never be put through to an answering service that asks us to 'hold until...'. All our prayers go to the same person at the same place—

'Our Father in heaven'—when we pray in the name of Jesus.

Praying with the Holy Spirit

We pray to God the Father through Jesus and with the help of the Holy Spirit. God knows us through and through. He knew that we would never be able to have the strength to love him 'with all your heart and with all your soul and with all your strength and with all your mind' (Luke 10:27) without help, so Jesus left his Holy Spirit to help us. This unseen Spirit of Jesus is our helper, guide and comforter. He is the one who enables us to say that Jesus is Lord (1 Corinthians 12:3).

The Holy Spirit is essential for our praying. He prompts us when to pray. He helps us know how to pray, and, when we are stuck and don't know what to pray for, he steps in (Romans 8:26–27). The Holy Spirit provides different gifts to help each Christian follow Jesus. One of these is a new heavenly language (also known as 'speaking in tongues'), which we can use to pray when ordinary words run out (1 Corinthians 14). One of my favourite descriptions of this says, 'Praying in tongues is what sometimes happens when God's love takes your breath away, and you're left with God's breath instead.'[1] This gift is widely used in some parts of the Church. Paul Yonggi Cho, a Korean pastor who for many years led one of the largest churches in the world, has often spoken of his reliance on the Holy Spirit, whom he calls his 'Senior Partner', and whom he consults before praying and making any sort of decision.

Prayer is a key

Prayer is also a key to understanding God's heart. Richard Foster movingly describes how God is longing to welcome us 'home'.

He invites us into the living room of his heart where we can put on old slippers and share freely. He invites us into the kitchen of his friendship where chatter and batter mix in good fun. He invites us into the dining room of his strength, where we can feast to our heart's delight. He invites us into the study of his wisdom where we can learn... and the workshop of his creativity... He invites us into the bedroom of rest where new peace is found, and where we can be naked and vulnerable and free.[2]

The key to this home—which is the heart of God—is prayer. Prayer not only enables us to talk to God about the things that concern us, but it also helps us to understand God better.

One of the most famous prayers, used in every denomination and across the world, is the Lord's Prayer, so called because Jesus taught it to his disciples when they asked him to teach them how to pray:

Our Father in heaven,
hallowed be your name.
Your kingdom come,
your will be done
on earth as in heaven.
Give us today our daily bread.

Forgive us our sins
as we forgive those who sin against us.
Lead us not into temptation
but deliver us from evil.
For the kingdom, the power
and the glory are yours,
now and for ever. Amen

The Lord's Prayer covers all the aspects of prayer that we will explore in this book. It starts with praising God for who he is and what he wants to do. Then we are told to ask for our own needs and the needs of others. Next we are challenged to confess our sins and whatever we may be holding against others and to ask for the strength to stand against temptation. And it ends as it starts, with praise and worship to God. It is a prayer that invites us to talk to God about the important things of life.

The more we discover about who God is and what he longs to see happen in his world, the better we are able to pray, as we shall explore in the following chapters.

- Prayer is not something we have dreamed up: we are created to be in touch with God. God invented prayer.
- Prayer is not simply saying the words or prayers at a set time, although having regular times of prayer, using written prayers, is one of the many ways we can pray.
- Prayer is not about trying to change God's mind. It is actually about us coming into line with his mind.
- Prayer is not a matter of reeling off a list of requests, although asking does form a very important part of prayer (see Chapter 7).

Instead, as some well-known practitioners of prayer have explained:

- Prayer is keeping company with God.[3]
- Prayer is to the spiritual life what the beating of the pulse and the drawing of the breath are to the life of the body.[4]
- Prayer is me being me in the presence of God being God.[5]

As we continue in our exploration of prayer, we need to look at an important question: why do we need to bother if God knows everything anyway?

A prayer

Father God, there is much about you I don't understand. Please help me to get to know you better. Amen

Getting started

* Take a few moments to stop.
* Pause and stop what you are doing. Relax. Make room for God.
* Presence: know that he is with you.
* Ponder Psalm 42:1–2: 'As the deer pants for streams of water, so my soul pants for you, O God. My soul thirsts for God, for the living God.'
* Picture the scene: think about the dry areas in your life. See yourself seeking and finding him. Speak to him in your heart.

* Promise: hold on to his promise as you reach out to him, remembering the words of the psalmist: 'Trust in him at all times, O people; pour out your hearts to him, for God is our refuge' (Psalm 62:8).

3 Why pray?

Does prayer have a place in our fast-paced society today? It would seem so.

When the television series *The Monastery* was first shown in the UK in 2005, it was so popular that it generated a new format of programming about prayer and spirituality, including *The Convent* and *The Retreat*. Many thousands of viewers contacted Worth Abbey, where the programme was made, to find out more about prayer and silence and to go on retreats. To quote from the Abbey's website:

Nowadays, many of us find ourselves saying that we are too busy, that we wished there were more hours in the day. For a healthy life, we all need moments and places of sanctuary... What more and more people are finding helpful is to adopt a simple framework which includes work, prayer and rest, both on one's own and with others.[1]

The Retreat Association confirms that its annual Quiet Weekend, 'Stop—in the name of God', has also been growing in popularity.[2]

This interest in prayer and spirituality was further confirmed by the research carried out by the Christian organization Tearfund for Global Poverty Week in November 2007. *Prayer in the UK*[3] revealed that prayer is a vital part of life for nearly half of UK adults. Two thousand British adults were surveyed, with 42 per cent saying that they pray (whether regularly or only in a crisis). This percentage is equivalent to around 20 million adults in the whole population. Of those 20 million, the survey suggests that 13 million pray at least once a month and 12.5 million at least once a week. Nearly nine million adults pray every day.

The survey also reveals strong belief in the power of prayer to bring about positive change in the world. One in three of all UK adults believes that God is watching over them and will answer their prayers; 12 million believe that prayer can change their friends', families' and their own lives. One in five believes that prayer changes the world.

It has also been interesting to see how the issue of prayer has been profiled in books and in the media. For example, the television and radio presenter John Humphrys recounts how he stopped going to church at the age of 15 when, as a young newspaper reporter in the Welsh valleys, he found church meaningless. In his autobiography he writes, 'Yet, I continued to pray. I prayed every single night without fail for half a century. The problem was that I had absolutely no notion of the God to whom I was supposed to be praying nor, for that matter, why I was praying.'[4]

As these examples show, people of all backgrounds are exploring prayer, and it would seem that more people are praying than are presently attending Christian churches across the UK.

But what is distinctive about how we as Christians pray? As the UK becomes increasingly secular, and confidence in the truths of the Christian faith is being challenged, we need to consider carefully questions such as 'Why do we need to pray if God knows everything anyway?' and 'Why would an all-powerful, all-knowing God need me to pray?'

So—why do we pray?

We pray because…

We start with the amazing fact that the God who created the universe actually wants us to come to know him better. We come back to what we explored earlier in Chapter 2—that prayer is all about relationship with a God of love who wants us to be in touch with him. When God revealed himself to me, I received love, affirmation, comfort, forgiveness and welcome, which has made such a difference to how I have gone about walking and talking with him over these past years. The whole story of the Bible is one in which we see God wanting people to live their lives connected with his plans and purposes. He constantly invites us to draw near and listen to him: 'Seek the Lord while he may be found; call on him while he is near' (Isaiah 55:6); 'Come to me, all you who are weary and burdened, and I will give you rest' (Matthew 11:28). And as we draw closer and start to pray, we discover more fully who we are.

We pray because God himself modelled in Jesus a life of prayer. Jesus did not say '*If* you pray', but '*When* you pray' (Matthew 6:5–7). He did not squeeze prayer into his life and ministry. He slotted his friendships, ministry and travelling in between times of prayer. Jesus needed to have time with his heavenly Father in order to keep in touch and to know what he should be doing.

If he did, so do we. If he needed to have time apart from the rat race, we need to do the same. Jesus was able to be so in tune with his Father because he made time for prayer.

We pray because the early Christians made prayer a priority in their worship, decision-making and mission—and its importance has been passed down the generations to this day.

We pray because our prayers matter to God. We may think that our prayer is too small to be noticed, but I take great comfort from Revelation 8:1–5, where we read that God halted the worship in heaven for half an hour so that the prayers of the saints (which means us!) could be heard, received and then sent back down to earth to make a difference.

God hears the prayers of every person. Jonathan Aitken found that to be true when he was admitted to Belmarsh Prison. He writes about how he felt on that first evening:

It seemed natural to turn to His divine power with a cri de coeur for help since, in the frightened loneliness of my cell, no earthly power was capable of offering me protection. So I knelt down on the concrete floor and tried to say a prayer. I remembered that just before going off to the Old Bailey to be sentenced, a friend had put into my pocket a calendar-style booklet entitled Praying the Psalms. *I turned to the page for June 8. It recommended Psalm 130, which began:*

Out of the depths I cry to you, O Lord
O Lord hear my voice.
Let your ears be attentive to my cry for mercy.

As I studied its eight short verses, a warm and comforting wave of reassurance flooded over me. Suddenly, I realized that I was not as lonely, scared, helpless or vulnerable as I had thought. The author of the psalm had been there before me.[5]

We pray because God wants to extend his kingly rule in his world and he has chosen us to work with him. In this partnership of friendship, God can do things through us that he could not do if we did not pray. He has chosen prayer to be a mighty weapon by which we can draw on his power and strength (see Chapter 10).

He wants to bring change—change firstly in ourselves. The more we find ourselves caught up in conversations with God and invite him to be part of our daily lives, the more we will find that our moods, our thoughts and our priorities are changed (Colossians 3:10). As the late Basil Hume once said, 'If people pray their consciousness becomes more selective. It is very difficult to be a praying person and then to go out and be beastly to our neighbour.'

God wants to bring change—through us to others. He is longing for us to be channels of his love, his peace and his healing and to enable all people to come to know his Son, Jesus Christ. Some time ago, I heard about a small church, which found itself in the position of having only 73 members, all of whom would be classed as 'older people'. They knew that the church would have to close unless something happened, so they decided to try prayer. They started to pray that ten new members would join in the next year. Within four months, seven new people had joined the church. By the end of the first year, 13 more had joined, including some young families. That story bears out Archbishop William Temple's words: 'People tell me that answers to prayer are merely coincidences. I can only reply that when I pray coincidences happen and when I stop praying they stop happening.'

We also pray when we are in desperate need and know that we have nowhere or no one else to turn to. A Bulgarian pastor, imprisoned for his faith under the old communist regime, said this:

Under such circumstances, the only thing no one can do is take away the opportunity to pray. I realized that when I needed prayer most, God deprived me of the chance to do anything else… In prison I came to know that God can satisfy our needs in two different ways—by giving us what we pray for and by delivering us from the need for which we pray… I was hungry for most of the time. Then I prayed, 'Lord, you fed five thousand people with five loaves of bread and two fish. Here there is only one of me, so even crumbs will be enough.' God did not give me more bread, but he did free me from the feelings of hunger… In prison I realized that we have the mightiest weapon given to us by God—prayer.

If prayer is so important to God, let's now look at how we can do it. There are many elements to prayer and we will look first at worship.

A prayer

Lord Jesus, I want to thank you for the gift of prayer. Please help me to want to bother to pray. Amen

Getting started

* Read John 4:1–30.

* Fill a glass or jug with water and find a place where you won't be disturbed. Read the passage again and start to sip the water. Continue to read through the passage, sipping the water, and stay until you have finished drinking all the water. Leave time and space for God to speak to you and refresh you with his life-giving water—the Holy Spirit.[6]

4 Prayer is worship

Worship lies at the very heart of what it means to be human, for every man, woman and child is created to worship God and enjoy his company for ever.[1] Worship is not something to do before we pray; worship in itself is prayer. But what do we mean by worship?

We worship as we praise and adore our God for who he is and what he has done (Psalm 95). We worship as part of our church culture when we meet together for services. We worship in and through our life when we are called to offer every area of our lives—our relationships, our time and our resources—to the Lord Jesus (Romans 12:1).

As God led his people through the wilderness and into the promised land, corporate worship became central for the Israelites. He taught them how to worship him—and it was different from the way the surrounding peoples worshipped their gods:

Break down their altars, smash their sacred stones and burn their Asherah poles in the fire; cut down the idols of their gods and wipe out their names from those places. You must not worship the Lord your God in their way. But you are to seek the place the Lord your God will choose from among all your tribes to put his Name there for his dwelling (Deuteronomy 12:3–5).

Worship, for the Israelites, was dependent on being in a certain place, either with the tabernacle in the desert or at the temple when it was built in Jerusalem, where they could offer sacrifices. As Israel became a nation, God raised up David as a leader, a man who loved to worship and praise his God. We find many of his hymns of prayer and praise in the book of Psalms: 'I will exalt you, my God the King; I will praise your name for ever and ever' (Psalm 145:1); 'Praise the Lord. Praise the Lord, O my soul. I will praise the Lord all my life; I will sing praise to my God as long as I live' (Psalm 146:1–2). On more than one occasion, he appointed special singers 'to sing joyful songs, accompanied by musical instruments: lyres, harps and cymbals' (1 Chronicles 15:16).

As the New Testament starts to unfold the story of Jesus, we find other examples of prayer as worship. When Elizabeth meets Mary, who is newly pregnant with Jesus, she pours out her heart in worship and prayer (Luke 1:42), and when Zechariah sees his son John born, he spontaneously starts to worship and pray (Luke 1:67). We find Jesus worshipping in prayer when the 72 disciples return to report back to him after being sent out on a short-term mission: 'I praise you, Father, Lord of heaven and earth, because you have hidden these things from the wise and learned, and revealed them to little children' (Luke 10:21).

In Jesus' day, the Jews traditionally worshipped with sacrifices at the temple and learnt about their faith in the synagogue. Access to God was determined by strict rules and regulations, but, as Jesus gave up his spirit on the day that has become known as Good Friday, we read, 'At that moment the curtain of the temple was torn in two from top to bottom' (Matthew 27:51). This was a powerful public sign of what was about to be revealed. Jesus had defeated death and given everyone free access to worship and pray to God anywhere. And we can look forward to the worship and praise in heaven. The book of Revelation gives us many glimpses of heaven, a place full of God's people praising and worshipping: 'Then I heard every creature in heaven and on earth and under the earth and on the sea, and all that is in them, singing: "To him who sits on the throne and to the Lamb be praise and honour and glory and power for ever and ever"' (Revelation 5:13).

As followers of Jesus, we need to learn how to become worshippers in all that we do, ready to praise our God for who he is and adore him for his love and mercy and faithfulness.

There are different ways to worship: we can worship with loud praise and singing and we can worship using simply silence and stillness. The Taizé Community in France[2] bears witness to the power of using worship, prayer and silence together. In 1940, a young Swiss man gathered a few friends around him and started a community founded on worship and prayer. Today many thousands of people visit each year and are profoundly blessed and renewed by time spent in an atmosphere of corporate and creative worship. Three times a day, everything on the hill of Taizé stops: the work, the Bible studies, the discussions. The bells call everyone to church for prayer. Young people from all over the world gather to pray and sing together with the brothers of the community.

At the International House of Prayer in Kansas City, USA, there has been unbroken praise and worship to God since September 1999, as teams of musicians, singers and pray-ers take it in turns to worship and praise and pray for their city, their nation and the world.[3]

I have attended many worship and prayer events over recent years, both in the UK and internationally, and they have all been different. I think of the time when we met up in Scotland to pray for the Group of Eight nations meeting (known as the G8) in July 2005. Many prayer meetings had been held before the actual G8 meeting, and during the three days of the G8 there were prayer gatherings around Scotland. The World Prayer Centre hosted an international prayer gathering as close as we could get to the hotel, at Gartmore House. It was clear in our first session that God, leading through his Holy Spirit, was asking us to concentrate on worship. For the next three days we spent much time using old hymns, new songs, scripture readings and silence to honour Jesus and to pray through the agenda. And when the news reached us of the London bombings, I remember that we stood in shocked silence and cried out to God for mercy, then returned to worship and prayer for all that was happening as the rescue effort began.

As individuals, we will find that we worship in contrasting ways because we all relate to God differently. What seems perfectly right for me may seem strange to you. Some Christians find it helpful to use symbols in worship. It may be a lighted candle to focus on Jesus 'the light of the world', or a vase of flowers or a single bloom to remind us to worship the Creator God. It may be a cross—hung on a wall or held in the hand—that helps us to meditate on what Jesus did for us. Some Christian traditions use icons, pictures that frame our thoughts and prayers. Other use prayer beads, or burn incense.

It is also good to use words, whether spoken or sung. Finding words to praise God should not be difficult: when we are talking with someone we love, we don't worry much about what we say; we just say it. In fact, if we are talking to a baby, we probably won't even use proper words. When we care deeply about a person, we will want to tell them of our love and appreciation. The book of Psalms is one of my favourite books in the Bible, as it gives me so many different words to praise and worship God.

When we do find it hard to praise God (and every one of us finds it hard sometimes), I think it helps if we ask God to show us why. It might have to do with our stubbornness and pride, when we just won't admit that we can't manage on our own. Or it could be because we are going through a crisis, illness or bereavement. Praising God has nothing to do with how we feel at any given time, but everything to do with who God is and the fact that he deserves our praise at all times.

As we are reminded in the letter to the Hebrews, we are to bring 'a sacrifice of praise' (Hebrews 13:15). I discovered a little about what that is like when, a few years ago, I gathered in Birmingham with 2000 Christians for a day to worship and pray for 'prodigals' (people we knew who had turned their backs on Christian faith). Many of us who went to that event did not particularly feel like praising God. We had come because we all had family members and loved ones who were living far from God. We spent much of the time in worship and prayer to our God who, we knew, was more concerned about our loved ones than we could ever be. He did indeed hear our sacrifice as the organizers later received many stories of prodigals who had come back to faith. In fact, that day of prayer prompted the leader of Care for the Family to write a book and set up a new ministry to encourage prayer for prodigals across the nation.[4]

How can we worship as we pray?

We can use the names of Jesus. The very familiar second line of the Lord's Prayer can trip off our tongues without our fully realizing its meaning. 'Hallowed be your name' (Matthew 6:9) means that God's name is being honoured or praised. There are many names for God in the Bible— more than enough for each day of the year.[5] For example, Jesus is almighty, bread, counsellor, deliverer, exalted, friend, great, holy, intercessor, judge, King of kings, Lord, Master, Name above all names, obedient, Prince of Peace, ruler, shepherd, teacher, understanding, vine and worthy. Each of these names tells us something about his character. By taking one and spending a few moments reflecting on what it means to us, we can praise God.

If we can't find the right words to use, I would recommend using the Bible, especially the book of Psalms. The writers of these wonderful praise songs so often seem to sum up exactly what I want to say. I have found it helpful to read a psalm every day, which is a discipline that I have kept for many years.

We can use music, even if we are not particularly musical. Sometimes I play a CD of Christian songs and allow myself to be caught up in praise and wonder; at other times I may pick up a hymn or song book and either sing or read the words. I like to have worship music playing as I do chores around the house, or on car or train journeys. My colleagues in the World Prayer Centre offices have worship music playing quietly for much of the time in our prayer room. It is interesting that *Songs of Praise* continues to attract high ratings, with an average of 4 million people watching each Sunday evening. And with technology advancing rapidly with our mobile phones, MP3 players, iPods and computers, it means that we can access music anywhere.

One of the most exciting prayer initiatives in recent years has been the Global Day of Prayer movement. This was started in 2005 when Christians from every country in Africa invited the world to join them on Pentecost Sunday to worship and pray for the nations, based on 2 Chronicles 7:14: 'If my people, who are called by my name, will humble themselves and pray and seek my face and turn from their wicked ways, then will I hear from heaven and will forgive their sin and will heal their land.' Here in the UK we have organized worship and prayer events in a variety of locations, including churches, cathedrals, parks, football stadiums and even a parliament building. On 11 May 2008 there were 214 nations participating (out of 220 nations in the world) in what was probably the biggest prayer meeting in the world. We held about 60 events across the UK—the largest being at Millwall football stadium in London— with around 11,000 people. The Global Day of Prayer vision links prayer, worship and mission together with a ten-day period of prayer and worship leading up to Pentecost, a day of united prayer on Pentecost Sunday, and then 90 days of blessing when all are encouraged to go out and share the good news in their communities. The Global Day of Prayer is set to continue through 2009, 2010 and beyond.[6]

However we choose to worship, we would do well to cultivate the habit of taking worship seriously. Just spending five minutes each day in God's presence, praising him for his love and faithfulness, can make a huge difference to the way we live our lives and help those around us, as this story illustrates.

Years ago, I worked for a training company. Often, I would go into my office and ask my secretary to hold my calls for ten minutes. I'd close the door, sit down at my desk and spend ten minutes adoring Jesus. On really rough days, I'd make it 20 minutes. On one particularly rotten morning, I was finishing a 20-minute session. I came out of my office to let my secretary know that I was ready to face calls when I heard her tell someone on the phone, 'Oh, you can't disturb him right now; he's worshipping.' And she wasn't a Christian! I looked at her, shocked. 'What did you say?' I asked. 'I told them you were worshipping,' she replied. 'How did you know?' 'I figured it out,' she said. 'I know you're a Christian, and I know that you go into that office stressed and come out totally different.'[7]

Worship, though, is only part of what prayer is about. We will now look at the next element of prayer: saying sorry, or 'confession'.

A prayer

Almighty God, you are so great and wonderful. Teach me how to worship you with the whole of my heart today and every day. Amen

Getting started

* Read Psalm 8.

* Go for a walk—in reality or in your imagination. Take a deep breath of fresh air, the air that sustains your life night and day, and open your mind and heart to take in the whole scene with your ears, eyes, nose and feet. Be aware of yourself, walking down the street or through a park. Listen to the sounds and to the silence. Use your eyes to enjoy the shape, depth, texture and movement in what is happening around you. Feel the touch of the air, rain, wind or sun on your skin; experience the feeling of the stone, grass or trees; smell the air. Continue to walk, looking, listening, smelling, tasting, feeling, using memory and imagination—all the time praising and thanking God for this world we live in. Let something speak to you, and stay with it for the rest of the day.

5 Prayer is saying sorry

If the prayer of praise is lifting our hearts to God, then the prayer of saying sorry, or confession, is opening our hearts to God.

Of all the different aspects of prayer, this is probably one of the most difficult. Which of us likes to admit we have done things wrong? You only have to be around children for a short time before something happens that requires an apology. After the tears have stopped, the pride has been conquered and those three special words 'I am sorry' uttered, everyone is happy as play resumes once again. If we think children find it hard, though, adults can find it far more difficult to admit that they have been wrong.

Sometimes we can be hesitant to pray because we know the true state of our hearts and our lives. That reticence is actually very appropriate, for God does know everything about us and all that we do wrong, but he simply wants us to come to him and confess our sins. Confession means acknowledging we have sinned, naming what we have done wrong and bringing it into God's presence. When we have done that, God can wipe away the sin and bring healing and reconciliation.

Jesus' moving story of the lost son makes this very clear (Luke 15:11–32). We meet the lost son first and see how he rejects his father's love and leaves home, taking his inheritance with him. But the glamour of his new lifestyle fades and the money eventually runs out. When he is reduced to being a pig-keeper (a particularly shameful occupation for a Jewish young man), he comes to his senses and decides to return home and apologize. His father is on the look-out for his return and, when he sees him coming, runs to meet him. As the lost son apologizes, his father welcomes him home to a banquet.

We are then introduced to the older son. As he watches all the attention being given to the younger son returning home, he becomes very jealous, so much so that the father has to reprimand him. The elder son is left with a difficult decision as to whether he can forgive his younger brother and be reconciled to both his father and his brother. God is always on the look-out for all his children to be in relationship with him, whether we are 'lost' or 'at home'.

Unconfessed sin stops prayer being answered, as the psalmist understood well: 'If I had cherished sin in my heart, the Lord would not have listened' (Psalm 66:18). Saying sorry to God helps us to keep in touch with him. As John writes, 'If we claim to be without sin, we deceive ourselves and the truth is not in us. If we confess our sins, he is faithful and just and will forgive us our sins and purify us from all unrighteousness' (1 John 1:8–9).

The story is told about a famous preacher, Smith Wigglesworth (1849–1947), who refused to pray for a sick woman in one of his meetings. When she asked him why, he told her it was because she had bitterness in her heart towards another woman in the service. She then went up to the other woman and gave her a formal handshake. Wigglesworth shouted, 'Woman, you will die of your sickness if you don't repent and make things right!' As 5000 people looked on, she began to sob and ask for forgiveness, and the other woman did the same. Suddenly it started to spread all through the crowd, and people began to forgive one another. Wigglesworth shouted again, 'Come on up and I will pray for you now.' She answered, 'You don't have to. God has just healed me.'

As we look at this in more depth, we do need to remember that Jesus bore our sins on the cross, once and for all time. We are forgiven—but we are still in need of being made more like Jesus.

How do we say sorry?

First, we come to God humbly and tell him what we know to be wrong in what we have said, done or thought. I usually find my own words work best. Sometimes I use simple words—for example, 'Lord, forgive me' or 'Lord, I'm sorry'—but at other times I need to spell out in more detail what has happened or is happening.

Second, we ask for his forgiveness. Jesus told a story of two men who went to the synagogue to pray—a Pharisee (a religious leader) and a tax collector (who would have been looked down on by the rest of society). The Pharisee prayed about how proud he was of himself and all that he did for others. The tax collector could only utter the words, 'God, have mercy on me, a sinner.' Jesus made it very clear that it was the humble prayer of the tax collector that was heard by God in heaven (Luke 18:10–14).

Using prayers that others have written can help me to frame what I want to say. One of the shortest and yet most profound is the Jesus Prayer, which can be said to the rhythm of our own breathing (a kind of prayer sometimes called a 'breathing prayer'). This is one of the oldest Christian prayers, formalized by the Orthodox Churches in the fifth century: 'Lord Jesus Christ, Son of God, have mercy on me, a sinner'. Today, the Jesus Prayer (or similar adaptations) is used by many Christians outside the Orthodox tradition.

Using prayers from the Bible can also help us find the right words to confess what is on our hearts. Once again, one of my favourite places to look is the book of Psalms, especially numbers 32, 38, 51 or 102. Alternatively, there are many books of prayers which can provide us with historic and modern prayers that others have written.[1]

Whatever words, prayers or books we use, it is helpful to aim to have a time each day before God when we take stock of what has happened and ask the Holy Spirit to show us where we need to say sorry. Saying sorry is, however, only part of the story.

Third, we need to ask God to help us change our attitudes and lifestyle, so that we continue to become more like him. True confession will lead to our turning round and changing direction—which is called 'repentance'. When Jesus called Zacchaeus the tax collector to become one of his followers, Zacchaeus' heart was changed. He immediately knew that he needed to stop what he was doing, so he offered to pay back all the money he had in effect stolen from his customers (Luke 19:8).

Fourth, we need to receive the cleansing that God offers. God in his love has made a way for us to receive forgiveness. We receive it by faith from a God who hears and answers our prayers. It sounds simple, and it is simple. We can find it helpful, however, to hear that forgiveness from somebody to whom we have confessed—for example, when the prayer of absolution is said by the service leader in the Anglican Church after the whole congregation together has confessed their sins.

Fifth, we need to forgive others, as the Lord's Prayer reminds us: 'Forgive us our sins, for we also forgive everyone who sins against us' (Luke 11:4). When Peter asked Jesus, 'How many times shall I forgive?' Jesus replied, 'Seventy-seven times', indicating that we need to keep forgiving and forgiving and forgiving. He went on to tell the story of an unforgiving servant, which clearly shows how forgiveness for our own sins is actually dependent on how we extend forgiveness to others (Matthew 18:21–35). As C.S. Lewis put it, 'To be a Christian means to forgive the inexcusable, because God has forgiven the inexcusable in you.'[2]

It is hard to pray for forgiveness, especially if we have been wronged. There have been several Christians who have openly talked about forgiveness in recent years. After the trial and conviction of Anthony Walker's killers in November 2005, his mother Gee, who is a Christian, shared very publicly about how she had forgiven his killers:

Why live a life sentence? Hate killed my son, so why should I be a victim too? Unforgiveness makes you a victim and why should I be a victim? Anthony spent his life forgiving. His life stood for peace, love and forgiveness and I brought them up that way. I have to practise what I preach.[3]

In March 2008, Jim Duell, the Christian father of murdered Ipswich prostitute Tania Nicol, revealed why he had to forgive her killer. He said, 'I forgive him. If I didn't, I would be consumed with anger and hatred. I'm not going to visit him in prison and make friends, but I made a decision to forgive him. It wasn't easy but it has helped me.'[4]

These stories remind me of the fact that unforgiveness affects all those involved and, unless we let go and forgive, our ability to move on will be severely limited.

Saying sorry is not confined to the individual. There are times when, as families or as a group of friends, we need to say sorry for things done and said against others and against God. On other occasions, groups of Christians from different churches may be called by God to respond together in asking for forgiveness. In 2001, church leaders in Stoke-on-Trent were faced with the results of a socio-economic study that highlighted their town as the worst place to live in the country. The leaders gathered and asked God for his help, then arranged another prayer gathering on the theme of 2 Chronicles 7:14: 'If my people, who are called by my name, will humble themselves and pray and seek my face and turn from their wicked ways, then will I hear from heaven and will forgive their sin and will heal their land.' As Debra Green tells the story:

This proved to be a powerful evening as 200 Christians gathered to cry out for God's mercy. Such was the impact of the event that similar united prayer gatherings started to take place each month under the banner of '2C7'... Some six years later, the 2C7 meetings are still going strong and have provided a platform for greater unity across the Body of Christ... As Christians have started to 'humble themselves, pray and seek God's face' for local education, political, crime and health needs, so we have begun to note a series of good news stories to emerge in these areas.[5]

Saying sorry and forgiving can also be done by whole people-groups and nations. I remember when, in 1983, not long before the Iron Curtain was lifted, Pope John Paul II visited his homeland of Poland. As thousands of people began to gather for a large open-air mass, they were organized to march in groups of parishes. It was reported that as they walked past the Communist Party Headquarters they chanted, 'We forgive you, we forgive you.' They maintained that spirit of forgiveness in spite of all the atrocities that were carried out against the Catholic Church. In time, the regime crumbled.

A prayer

Loving Father, I know I am not always honest with you or myself. I am sorry. Please forgive me and help me to start again. Amen

Getting started

* Write your own breathing prayer. It should be short, around seven or eight syllables long. The first three or four syllables are prayed as you inhale, the others as you exhale. It will include a name for God and will end with a request, along the lines of the traditional Jesus Prayer. Richard Foster suggests the following method.

Find some uninterrupted time and a quiet place and sit in silence, being held in God's loving presence. After a few moments allow God to call you by name… Next, allow this question to surface: 'What do you want?' Answer this question simply and directly. Maybe a single word will come to your conscious mind: 'peace', 'faith', 'strength'. Perhaps it will be a phrase: 'to understand your truth', 'to feel your love'. Next, connect this phrase with the most comfortable way you have of speaking about God: 'blessed Saviour', 'Abba', 'Immanuel', 'Holy Father', 'gracious Lord'. Finally, you will want to write out your breath prayer, staying within what is comfortable for you to say in one breath.[6]

6 Prayer is giving thanks

Thanksgiving should be one of the strongest motivations to pray, as we are able to express our gratitude to God for what he has done for us. We worship God for who he is, and we give thanks for what he has done. This follows on naturally from praise and confession.

Thanksgiving has been a central part of worship down the centuries. God ordained that the 'thank offering' would be an integral part of the worship of ancient Israel (Leviticus 7:12). When David heard from the Lord that his son Solomon was to build the temple, he made Solomon king of Israel. David then appointed 4000 Levites 'to praise the Lord with the musical instruments… provided for that purpose' (1 Chronicles 23:5). 'Give thanks to the Lord, for he is good; his love endures for ever' is a familiar refrain in the Old Testament (see, for example, 2 Chronicles 5:13; 20:21; Psalm 106:1; 107:1). When the wall at Jerusalem was rebuilt, Nehemiah assigned large choirs to give thanks (Nehemiah 12:31).

The same note of thanksgiving is carried into the New Testament. Mary gave thanks as she willingly accepted the role of being the mother of Jesus (Luke 1:46–55). Simeon thanked God when he met the baby Jesus and realized that he was indeed the long-awaited Saviour (2:25–32). Before Jesus gave out the five loaves and two fishes to feed the five thousand, he 'gave thanks and broke' the loaves (9:16). One of the most poignant references is at the end of Luke's Gospel, when the risen Jesus, after walking with Cleopas and his friend, is invited to have a meal with them. We read that 'he took bread, gave thanks, broke it and began to give it to them' and they recognized who he was (24:30). Thanksgiving was a hallmark of the early Church. In his writings, Paul is constantly either thanking God for his brothers and sisters in Christ (Romans 1:8) or encouraging his readers to be thankful (Ephesians 4:20).

Is it possible to be thankful when life seems to be against us and we find ourselves in the middle of pain and suffering? Paul poses two challenges: give thanks *for* all circumstances (Ephesians 5:20) and give thanks *in* all circumstances (1 Thessalonians 5:18). No matter what we are going through, he encourages us to give thanks to the God who is over every circumstance that we face. We do not thank him for the adverse or painful circumstances themselves, but we place the situations and people into his hands and, in faith, trust him for the outcome. We often cannot do much to change things, but we can cry out to God who can bring change. And the result? We can then be given the strength to cope with what we have to face and can be prevented from becoming cruel, angry or bitter.

When I meet people who are going through suffering, bereavement or illness, I usually find it easy to recognize those who are seeking to trust God in the midst of the pain. I think of a family who moved to Canada so that the husband could do a three-year postgraduate study programme. Shortly after they arrived, first his wife and then one of his children were diagnosed with cancer. During the long hard months of treatment that followed, what kept them going as a family was a daily time with God to draw on his strength and love.

However, the reality is that many of us find saying 'thank you' difficult or even impossible—and this affects God. When Jesus heals ten lepers, there is a real sense of his disappointment when only one remembers to thank him (Luke 17:11–19). This was powerfully brought home to me a number of years ago, when a group of us acted out this passage in a drama workshop. After prayerfully reading through the text, ten of the group chose to be lepers and I was put in the role of Jesus. The group acted out how they would have been affected by leprosy. As I approached them, they cried out, 'Lord, have mercy on us!' and I in turn said, 'Go and show yourselves to the priest.' I found that my heart sank as they walked off 'healed', and I was so pleased when one did come back. As we talked about it afterwards, it was interesting to find that all nine felt guilty that they had not said 'thank you'. It reminded them of how often they failed to thank God and it showed me afresh that he does mind if we are ungrateful.

What do we give thanks for?

We should be thankful for the past and should pause to remember how God has been faithful as we look back on our own lives and those of our families, friends, church and nation. We will find ourselves giving thanks for God's goodness, for the 'indescribable gift' of Jesus (2 Corinthians 9:15), for his offer of forgiveness and for the gift of the Holy Spirit.

We should be thankful for the present—right up

to today. Most of us in the developed world take our everyday luxuries of food, home, water, clothes, health and money for granted. It can be helpful to ask the question, 'What am I grateful for today?' and to respond in prayer accordingly.

We should also be thankful for the future. While we do not know what the long-term future holds, we do know that Jesus has gone before us and that our future is safe in his hands. Rather than worrying about the future, we ought instead to turn our concerns into prayers of thanksgiving. Paul wrote to the church in Philippi, 'Do not be anxious about anything, but in everything, by prayer and petition, with thanksgiving, present your requests to God. And the peace of God, which transcends all understanding, will guard your hearts and your minds in Christ Jesus' (Philippians 4:6–7).

We can encourage the habit of giving thanks by adopting a simple daily routine. For example, we can pause to give thanks as we get up in the morning, make a cup of coffee, turn the computer on or off, work through a pile of ironing or end a phone call. There is a long Christian tradition of taking time at the end of the day to stop and reflect back as well as looking ahead (sometimes called the Prayer of Examen, or reviewing the day). In this simple prayer exercise, we are encouraged to find a quiet place, look back over the day and recall what we are thankful for, then turn that recollection into praise and prayer. We then reflect on what might not have gone so well, offering it to God for his cleansing and guidance for the day ahead.

If you find that your prayer life has become stuck, try

spending your prayer time in thanksgiving. When I have done that, I find it totally changes my perspective on life and enriches my conversations with God. I remember a friend of mine sharing how an African pastor had visited his church and challenged the congregation to think of five things for which they were thankful to God, before they got out of bed in the morning. As people followed his advice, my friend described how it began to transform their perception of God and what he did for them daily.

As we are learning, prayer is about worship, saying sorry, giving thanks and asking (the subject of our next chapter). All these facets are so intertwined that it is often impossible to separate them. As we begin a conversation with God, we might start with praise, find ourselves prompted to say sorry and then begin to ask in prayer, stopping in the middle to thank him for something that we have just remembered. Equally, we could start by thanking him and move on from there. There can be no formula or system to a relationship that is developing as the days, months and years go by.

A prayer

Our Father in heaven, thank you for loving me, for caring for me, for forgiving me. Help me to become a thankful and grateful person. Amen

Getting started

* Reviewing the day (the Prayer of Examen): this simple prayer exercise can be done at any time and helps us to see how God has been at work in the details, the moods and the feelings of the day. It need only take about ten minutes.

* We should be in a place where we can focus on God. Start by playing back the events of the day in any order and look first at the moments you enjoyed. Relive them, relish them and thank God for them. Then ask the Lord to remind you of your moods and inner feelings during the day. Moods and inner feelings usually come from our desires, and our habitual desires become attitudes. When desires/attitudes are satisfied, we are content; when they are frustrated, we become irritable. Were my desires/attitudes directed to his kingdom? Am I living to praise, reverence and serve God or are my desires directed to my personal world? Ask forgiveness for not responding to God in the events of the day—and allow yourself to receive it. Ask his guidance for tomorrow and entrust yourself to his goodness.

7 Prayer is asking

We come now to the next part of prayer—asking, or, as it is sometimes called, supplication. I know that many of us find asking difficult, especially if we are British! Can I really pray for myself? Surely that is selfish? We are sometimes reticent about praying for others: might we be interfering? In any case, do I have the right to pray for someone else? What if I pray the wrong thing?

Incredible as it may seem, asking is at the heart of our relationship with God because he has made it this way. As the 19th-century preacher Charles Spurgeon said, 'Asking is the rule of the kingdom.' When a child comes up to you with a big smile and asks you to help them, what do you feel? I know I am pleased that they want my help. It is the same with God. He is pleased when we come and ask him.

Learning from Jesus

We can take encouragement from Jesus in his life of prayer. We know that he asked for help from his heavenly Father when he was on earth. For example, he prayed before his baptism, before choosing the twelve disciples and before he went to the cross. In coming to his Father and asking for guidance, Jesus was ensuring that he was in line with God's plans for him. We need to do the same and be honest before God about what we need in terms of our practical and spiritual life. We daily need forgiveness and help in all sorts of ways; we need the guidance of the Holy Spirit and wisdom to use our time and our lives in his service.

Jesus prayed for others. He prayed for Peter, that his faith would endure (Luke 22:32), and he prayed for all his disciples and for all those who would believe after them (John 17). If praying in this way was important for Jesus, it is even more important for us.

Jesus also taught about the need to ask and be persistent in prayer, telling the following story to sum up what this means. A friend opens his home at midnight to a hungry traveller, who has been on a long journey. Out of courtesy, the friend must feed this traveller, but he finds that there is no bread in the house. So he goes to the house of another friend, knocks hard on the door and wakes him up. This man is not best pleased but in the end he has no choice but to get up and give his friend the bread (Luke 11:5–8). Jesus ends with a beautiful promise to encourage us in our praying: 'Ask and it will be given to you; seek and you will find; knock and the door will be opened to you' (v. 9). In the original Greek, those words convey a stronger meaning, which I have often missed: they mean ask and go on asking, seek and go on seeking, knock and go on knocking. We are like the friend in the middle who is not able to meet the needs of his hungry traveller but knows someone who can. As we continue to pray and ask, God is able to intervene.

That isn't the end of the story! Jesus goes on to add, 'Which of you fathers, if your son asks for a fish, will give him a snake instead? Or if he asks for an egg, will give him a scorpion? If you then, though you are evil, know how to give good gifts to your children, how much more will your Father in heaven give the Holy Spirit to those who ask him!' (vv. 11–13). Again Jesus lays out clearly just what our lovely heavenly Father is like—waiting to give good gifts to us, his children.

Asking in prayer for others

As that story illustrates, God wants us to pray for others. As we pray for them, we put ourselves in the position of standing in the gap between them and God and we then ask God to help them. This form of prayer is called intercession (a term used in a court of law to mean mediating and pleading for a case). Intercession always has a close connection with the cross and resurrection. The supreme act of intercession was on the cross when Jesus stood between us in our sinfulness and God in his holiness, and it cost him his life. This is what Jesus does for us as our heavenly high priest: 'he always lives to intercede' for us (Hebrews 7:25).

I have found the following illustration very helpful. Picture a person in one room of a house and God in the next room. Between the two there is a wall, but if you stand in the doorway connecting the two rooms, you can see them both. The person and God could each speak to the other through you. When you find yourself in touch with someone who needs God's help, you become the contact between the two. Your prayers connect that person's need with God's power. That is intercessory prayer.

Intercessory prayer is part of everyone's role as a Christian and is a powerful way of loving and caring for others; there is, in fact, no greater privilege. James says, 'The prayer of a righteous person is powerful and effective' (James 5:16). As we pray, we need to remember that we ask in the name of Jesus (John 14:13; see Chapter 1 of this book) and we ask from the place of being 'at home' with Jesus (John 15:17, THE MESSAGE).

What should we ask for?

A good place to start is to ask God and find out what he wants. So often, we rush in with our own shopping lists and we forget to stop and to listen (see Chapter 8). At the heart of intercessory praying is learning to tune into what is on God's heart, by listening, waiting, asking and then praying.

We can learn much from the story of Abraham interceding for Lot, in Genesis 18. At the beginning of the chapter, Abraham receives three unexpected visitors. As he gives hospitality to them, and makes room for God to stop and rest, God is able to ask some very penetrating questions that challenge Abraham's reluctance to believe that God would ever fulfil the promise of a son (he and Sarah had been waiting for about 25 years). As the story unfolds, we see how, because of the growing relationship between Abraham and his God, God is able to reveal what is in his heart about the city of Sodom. Abraham's faith is strengthened and he begins to intercede for Lot and the city of Sodom until God relents and extends his mercy towards the city. In the next chapter it is interesting to see how God answers Abraham's heartfelt prayers for Lot by sending two angels to rescue him and his family. Intercessory prayer means listening to God and shaping our prayers in line with his purposes.

We can ask God to reveal his purposes by using the same questions that we might ask another person. Who do you want me to pray for? What do you want me to ask for? Why is such and such happening? What's in the way? What is your will for that person in this situation? Why is nothing apparently happening? What do you want me to do next?

We can always pray about everyday basic needs for ourselves and others, like health, food, clothes, relationships and finance, as in the Lord's Prayer: 'give us each day our daily bread' (Luke 11:3). Many have found the acronym BLESS (an approach originally developed by Indian Christians) a useful framework for prayer for friends, family and neighbours. When we ask God to bless another person, we are in effect asking God to give them all of his love, peace, joy and help. Working through each letter of the word BLESS means that we cover every aspect of their life, as follows:

- **Body and health**: pray for all physical needs.
- **Labour**: pray for work, unemployment, finance issues, retirement.
- **Emotional**: pray for joy, peace and relief from stress.
- **Social**: pray for relationships at every level—home, family, friends and work.
- **Spiritual**: pray for a deepening of faith, holiness and the need for repentance.

We can pray for God's will to be 'done on earth as it is in heaven' (Matthew 6:10). This is where we ask that the whole of a person's life (use of time, finance, relationships and everything else) is submitted totally to his will. I usually start with a time of praying for myself and then move on to pray for those closest to me. Then, if time permits, I pray more widely, for my church, my workplace and maybe an item in the news. We need to learn to start in our own backyard and move out, led by the Holy Spirit, just as a pebble dropped into water sends ripples to fill the whole pond.

Whom should we pray for?

Paul, writing to Timothy, said:

I urge, then, first of all, that requests, prayers, intercession and thanksgiving be made for everyone—for kings and all those in authority, that we may live peaceful and quiet lives in all godliness and holiness. This is good, and pleases God our Saviour, who wants all people to be saved and to come to a knowledge of the truth (1 Timothy 2:1–4).

Paul is saying that we should pray for everyone—that he wants everyone to come to know Jesus.

How can we do that? Research in the United States has shown that individuals tend to pray for one of four categories: people, issues, events and communities (although it is my experience that we often pray for things in all four areas). Some people will concentrate on praying for people—family, friends, neighbours, colleagues, missionaries or leaders in their church, community or nation. For instance, there are a number of Christian groups who regularly put on prayer breakfasts for their local MPs in towns and cities around the UK. Once or twice a year, these church leaders invite key leaders in their communities, including MPs, to meet with praying Christians, so that the Christians can hear from them first-hand what pressures they face and learn how to pray for them.

Other people may be more concerned with issues such as children, education, abortion, homelessness or poverty. One group, Churches Together Schools Team, works with 17 schools in Kent:

We pray for staff and pupils and to support Christians within the schools. A school's openness to your praying for them comes out of having a good relationship with them, and the boldness to say, 'As Christians we believe prayer is important. Would you like us to pray for you?' We've been able actually to go into the staff room to pray when there's been a tragedy in the life of the school, or pray over the children during an assembly. And prayers are answered! We've had comments like, 'I don't know what happened, but we appointed just the right person to that post.'[1]

Others will be prompted to pray for issues facing their communities. For example, across the UK there are many initiatives helping churches link up to pray for and work with their local police forces.[2] The Lincolnshire Police Association has launched a Police Watch, which communicates urgent prayer requests to those involved. Another initiative has focused on the road fatality rate, which is one of the highest in the country. After consistent prayer, started in 2002 by Lincs in

Prayer, a marked fall has been seen in the number of people seriously injured and those killed. (In 2002 there were 739 seriously injured and 104 fatalities, and, in 2006, 330 seriously injured and 64 fatalities.[3])

During the Welsh revival at the beginning of the 20th century, one of the leaders of this extraordinary move of God, Evan Roberts, was asked what was the secret. 'There is no secret,' he replied. 'Ask and you shall receive.' The challenge for us is to do just that.

A prayer

Loving Lord, please forgive me when I am slow to ask. Help me to be bold, persistent and wise so that your name may be glorified. Amen

Getting started

* Use the acronym BLESS to pray for a neighbour today.

* Use your hand. Your fingers can be used to bring to mind different things to pray for:

* **Thumb:** this is the strongest digit on your hand. Give thanks for the strong things in your life, such as home and family, relationships that support and sustain you.

* **Index finger:** this is the pointing finger. Pray for all those people and organizations in your life who guide and help you—friends, teachers, doctors, nurses, emergency services and so on.

* **Middle finger:** this is the tallest finger. Pray for all who have power in the world, like world leaders and

their governments, members of parliament and local councillors and the Royal Family.

* **Ring finger:** this is the weakest finger on your hand. It cannot do much by itself. Remember the poor, the weak, the helpless, the hungry, the sick, the ill and the bereaved.

* **Little finger:** this is the smallest and the last finger on your hand. Pray for yourself.

8 Prayer is listening

Much of what we have looked at to do with prayer has focused on our talking to God—giving him praise and thanks, asking for his forgiveness and offering specific prayers for ourselves and others. We can easily make the mistake of thinking that prayer is just talking to God, but it takes two to have a conversation. We need to learn how to listen to God and receive from him, and so learn how best to pray for ourselves and for others. Prayer is not a monologue but a dialogue.

How does God speak?

I believe that God speaks both 'in' us and 'to' us in a variety of ways. During my 30 years as a disciple of Jesus Christ, there have been many times when I have had a sense that he is speaking 'in' me, when he brings back into my mind something that I have previously talked about, read about, or heard that is relevant to the situation I have been facing. But there have also been times when I have sensed God speaking to me in an audible voice.

I have learnt that God speaks through the Bible, a book written down many centuries ago and inspired by his Holy Spirit. When certain passages of scripture are read, we can have a real sense that God is speaking to us as old truths are brought home in new ways or we are again made aware of how much God loves us. Once, just before starting a daunting new job, I was reading the story of David going to fight Goliath (1 Samuel 17:39–

49). When I came to the part where David determines to go on trusting in God and not in the armour that Saul has lent him, I realized that this applied to me in my situation.

God may speak through other people. It may be someone you know well or someone you have just met, who, in the middle of a conversation, will speak words that help, guide, comfort or challenge you. God may also speak through dreams, as he did to Joseph (Matthew 1:20) and the magi (2:12), or visions, as he did to John on the island of Patmos (Revelation 1:12–18). Today, in nations of the world where it is not possible to talk openly about the Christian faith and Christians are being persecuted, many hundreds are turning to follow Jesus. When asked why, many reply that they have seen Jesus in a dream.

Many people find that we can hear God speak through the beauty of creation, or through a gut feeling, a nudge or a sense of something not being right in an event or a conversation.

God may also speak through books and sermons, an article in the press, a programme on the TV or radio, or through day-to-day events. I was recently at a *Redeeming our Communities* conference. The leadership team described how, while they were travelling to the venue, the oil warning light came on in the car and they had to stop and put in more oil. This surprised them as the car had recently been serviced and the oil levels had been checked before the journey. When they arrived and shared their sense that God was trying to get our attention, we stopped and prayed together. Many of us had a strong sense that it was the Holy Spirit nudging us to pray for each other to be filled up with more of the fullness of God (Ephesians 3:19). As this was shared with the conference, there was a general agreement and, as a result, a number of the speakers spontaneously ended their sessions by giving opportunities for people to receive prayer.

God wants us to hear him. Jesus clearly taught that his followers can know his voice and follow him, as sheep know the voice of their shepherd (John 10:27). But how do we learn to listen?

Make friends with stillness

To really listen to someone else, I need to be able to put down my own agenda and focus with all my energy on what the other person is saying, whether it is in a face-to-face conversation, over the phone or via a letter or email. I need to make time and give time.

If we want to learn how to listen to what God is saying, we need to make friends with stillness. In Psalm 46:10, God tells the psalmist, 'Be still, and know that I am God.' I imagine that this gave him a profound sense of the presence of God in whatever upheaval was happening around him at the time.

Learning to be still can be a challenge in our busy lives. The Abbot of Worth Abbey in Sussex writes:

I have recently taken to asking those who come to the monastery on retreat where they find sanctuary [sacred space] in their lives today. Some of them admit frankly that they do not have any sanctuary; they are just too busy... This busy-ness is so endemic that even the act of coming on retreat for forty-eight hours evokes in them strong feelings of guilt.[1]

Those who make time for stillness find it very beneficial, as Delia Smith shares: 'I make sure that I have two periods of total stillness and silence every day—once in the early morning and once in the evening for about 40 minutes. I'm lucky because I live in the country so I can be absolutely silent and still.'[2] A good way to start this practice is to take five minutes for stillness at the start and end of the day.

Meditate on the Bible

Meditation on God's word, the Bible, is like chewing food which, when digested, becomes part of us. We can learn to meditate when we read scripture by asking the Holy Spirit to speak to our hearts. There are different ways to pray using the Bible, besides carefully reading and seeking to understand what it is saying. We can pray through each verse and personalize it—for example, using a psalm. When reading any of the four Gospels, we can imagine Jesus by our side, speaking those words to us today, and take time to see how they might apply to us, talking to God about our answers. (For example, try reading Matthew 5:13–14; Mark 8:34–38 or John 14:1–4.)

Another method that I have found helpful is meditative or slow reading of Bible passages (also known as *lectio divina*). This has proved to be a wonderful tool, which has helped me to learn how to stop, listen and allow God's word to seep into my heart, mind and soul.

With this ancient method, we read the text slowly over and over again with a listening spirit (*lectio*). Then we reflect on what we are reading (*meditatio*). We pray in response to what we are picking up from our reading (*oratio*) and then move into resting in God's love (*contemplatio*). From there we seek to go out and share Christ with the people we meet. Mark's Gospel is a good starting point. This way of reading and praying is gaining in popularity and there are a number of books that can help us to develop the method.[3]

Make friends with silence

A great French saint of the 19th century, Jean-Baptiste Vianney, known as the *Curé d'Ars* (the parish priest of the village of Ars), noticed an old farm worker who used to come into his church and just sit there. One day he asked the man what he was doing while he sat in church, and the reply was, 'I look at him, and he looks at me, and we understand one another.'

That story shows us another kind of prayer, known as contemplative prayer, which is not so much about words and activism as about being silent in the presence of God. It is for anyone who wishes to explore a deeper understanding of God and his love for them and for his world. One way to get started in this way of prayer is to find a place where you will not be interrupted, and where you can sit or lie down. Then consciously relax your whole body, allowing your mind to calm down, so that you become more aware of God's presence. I find it helpful to start with a verse of scripture—for example, using one of my favourite promises from the Bible, which reminds me of God's love and faithfulness: 'Fear not, for I have redeemed you; I have summoned you by name; you are mine' (Isaiah 43:1b). As you open yourself to God, reach out in love. Surrender your concerns, hand over your sins, receive his forgiveness and remain in an attitude of listening silence. You may find you want to express praise. You may pray for others. You may just want to rest in him.

Whether we pray with others or on our own, it can be very helpful to allow silence to invade our personal space as we listen to God, who is in us and around us (Psalm 62:5). It can take a while to get into the discipline of being able to stop, relax, tune in to God and listen in this way, but the benefits make the effort worthwhile.

I have begun to use this type of praying more and more in recent years. I can also recommend taking time out to go on a prayer retreat for half a day, a whole day or longer, or finding a quiet garden in which to stop and enjoy silence.[4]

Prayer-walk

Prayer-walking is praying 'on site with insight', when we ask God to help us to see, hear and feel things that we do not normally pick up when we rush from place to place.

It is not difficult and can be done by anyone, anywhere, at any time. We can prayer-walk on our own or with others. Before starting, it is good to ask the Holy Spirit to cleanse our hearts and guide our steps. And as we prayer-walk, we need to keep our eyes open, listening to God and using what is seen to prompt prayer. For example, when we walk past the houses in our street and notice toys in a garden, we can pray for the children. If we see a boarded-up window, we can pray for God's light to penetrate into that house. If we see litter or graffiti, we can ask for God's cleansing love to come and be revealed to all who live in that area. After completing a prayer-walk, it is helpful to make a note to share with others (in your family, friends, home group or church) about what you have seen and prayed for.

Even if it is not possible to go out physically, we can use a map, search Google Earth for the area or use our imagination to walk down any road, or through any community or workplace, and lift to God the needs that come to mind. I recently heard of a town where Christians prayer-walked to almost all of the 70 churches in one month, with the aim to bless what God was doing in each place. One of the prayer-walkers commented, 'It was a stimulating experience where I gained a new appreciation of churches that I had not visited before.'

Prayer-walking can be a very powerful form of prayer. One of the most remarkable answers to prayer that I have heard about came from a group that was prayer-walking in Gloucester. As they came to a certain road, they felt a great sense of pain and sorrow. They were led to ask the Lord to reveal whatever was hidden in that place. It later turned out to be the site of many murders, as Fred and Rosemary West were brought to justice.

Listen through the news

Every day we hear news stories that can both encourage and discourage us. It could be local news from the radio, newspaper or your parish magazine, or national and international situations and disasters. How can we pray? Here are some suggestions that others have found helpful. You could spend some time in silence before the computer, TV or radio, asking for the Lord to have mercy. You could spread open the newspaper on the table or floor, light a candle and sit with the story. You could imagine yourself into the situation and pray from that viewpoint. You can pick out an individual—one of the people affected, the leader of a nation, an aid or relief worker, a Christian in that region—and pray for them.[5]

Listen to those we meet

As we learn to listen to God, we learn to pray as he prompts. A good friend of mine is passionate to help people learn about Jesus Christ. She is also someone who loves to pray and likes to make cakes! When she hears that someone has moved into the area, she calls round with a note on behalf of the church and a cake to welcome them into the community. If she hears about other issues—it could be an illness or it could be a celebration—she makes cakes and takes them round. As she is welcomed into many homes, she listens very carefully to what is being said and to the way the Holy Spirit is prompting her in her conversation. She returns home and prays for the needs she has heard about. As relationships develop, she is able to offer to pray for those she meets in their homes. The good news of Jesus has been shared and understood in many hearts in that community because of one person's willingness to take time to listen.

When the leader of Community Watchmen Ministries

was listening to a talk by a leading police officer in Merseyside, despairing at the levels of drug taking in the community and asking what could be done, she was prompted to offer to help by mobilizing prayer and starting Drugs Net.[6] Over recent years, Drugs Net has established a network of praying people across the region and provides specific prayer requests, often supplied by the Merseyside Police. Regular prayer bulletins are sent out and the leaders work closely with different parts of the police force across Merseyside. One of their newsletters stated, 'God answers our prayers—thank God for gun crime figures released by the Home Office [which] show Merseyside had an eight per cent decrease in gun crime; also a gang that used cross-channel ferries to smuggle £10m of drugs to Merseyside has been jailed for a total of 68 years.' CWM has been the catalyst for similar projects elsewhere in the UK.

None of these stories could have been told had Christians not been listening to God.

A prayer

Lord Jesus, how I long to be able to hear your voice today. Please still my heart and mind and help me to listen to you. Amen

Getting started

* Take a favourite passage of scripture and allow yourself
  time for some 'divine reading' (*lectio divina*). First, we
  need to slow down and open our minds and hearts to
  God. Second, we ask him to lead us by his Holy Spirit
  as we read a short passage of scripture at least two or
  three times, stopping to reflect as a thought, verse,
  word or idea emerges as a particular focus. Third,
  we respond in prayer as God leads—which might be
  prayer for ourselves or for others. If it is a verse of
  scripture that emerges, it is good practice to memorize
  it or make a note of it for future reference. Fourth, we
  allow ourselves the luxury of sitting with God for a
  while, enjoying his company.

9 Prayer is joining with others

It could be very easy to think that prayer is just something we do on our own, especially as we live in such an individualistic culture, but nothing could be further from the truth. In fact, there is no such thing as 'solitary' prayer. As we pray, we join with God and Jesus Christ, linked by the Holy Spirit, who helps us to cry '*Abba*, Father' (Romans 8:15). Even if we are physically on our own, we are never alone in spirit as Jesus is always with us: 'And surely I am with you always, to the very end of the age' (Matthew 28:20).

If we look at the Lord's Prayer, we find it is a corporate prayer. It starts by saying 'Our Father', not 'my Father', and continues with 'give us our daily bread', 'forgive us our sins' and 'lead us not into temptation'. Jesus also taught about the importance of agreement and unity in prayer when 'two or three come together in my name' (Matthew 18:19–20). The early Church put his teaching into practice and the disciples made prayer together a priority (Acts 2:42–47). As they sought the Lord and the power of his Holy Spirit, the Church grew and spread through the world.

Praying with others is one of the most exciting and encouraging ways to pray—and there are so many ways to do it!

Pray where you live

When I lived in community houses, regular times of fellowship around the table and times of prayer for each other were a real highlight of the week. I have been in many homes over the years where prayer has been an important part of life together, whether in a family or shared home context. I think of one family who put the names of their friends in a prayer pot and, at meal times, they all take out a slip of paper and pray together around the meal table.

Pray in small groups or prayer triplets

Most churches have small groups—Bible study, home or cell groups—that encourage those who come to pray for issues within and outside the group. Some churches have specific prayer groups that focus on praying for different aspects of the church's mission.

One of the most popular ways of praying together for friends who are not yet Christian has been in groups of three, known as prayer triplets. Prayer triplets were first started in preparation for Billy Graham's *Mission England* in 1986 and are based on Jesus' teaching on the importance of two or three agreeing in prayer. These three people (or three couples) meet together regularly to pray for three friends each who are not yet believing Christians. They have proved to be very effective in helping Christians to pray for and care for their not-yet Christian friends.

Pray in church services and at prayer meetings

While each denomination has different styles of worship, most include a time of corporate prayer in their services, often led from the front. During this time of prayer, I find it helpful to concentrate my thoughts on the words being said (some people repeat them silently, so as to make them their own) or picture in my mind the person or situation being prayed for.

The local church prayer meeting is another place to meet with others to pray. While not every church in Britain has a regular prayer meeting, many still do. Like many larger churches, Holy Trinity Brompton in London has adopted a simple strategy of having a number of different meetings throughout the week, each at a different time with a specific focus, which enables many to join in.

As a more recent development in many towns and cities, there are regular interchurch prayer groups to pray for specific issues that affect the whole community. For example, there are several initiatives mobilizing prayer for schools. One is the Schools Prayer Network, run by CARE, which encourages anyone connected with a school to form a prayer group. There have been some very specific answers to prayer:

One inner-city secondary school had a serious financial crisis, facing a debt of £200,000. The prayer group was informed about this by the Christian teacher who coordinated it, and they got on their knees. A term later the news came back that the local authority had agreed to help, the bursar had done some skilful budgeting and the shortfall had turned into a surplus.[1]

The challenge of praying with others

Although praying with others can be rewarding and exciting, it can seem quite daunting to join in with such groups. There are a number of reasons for this.

First, as we pray on our own, we develop our own ways of talking with God, and it can be a shock when we move from that intimacy with God to praying with others. We need to appreciate that we all pray differently. Some people like to use written prayers, others like to pray using their own words (called extempore prayer) and others prefer to pray in silence. As a group of people get to know each other, however, it is amazing how the different ways of praying can be blended together.

Second, we need to recognize that some people feel daunted when praying in a larger group. We have to remind ourselves that we are not there to please ourselves but to please our heavenly Father. He is prompting us by his Spirit to pray; we have to follow his leading. Others may feel that they never say the right words, or find that their prayer has just been said by someone else. If someone else prays for what you were about to pray for, be encouraged that you have been led to pray for the same thing, and go ahead and pray your prayer. As you pray, others will then be able to pick up and stay with that topic until the Lord leads the prayer on to something else. If you feel nervous, why not turn to your Bible or service book and pray a prayer from there, or write your own prayer to read out during the meeting?

Third, one of the most common difficulties is simply not being able to hear what others are praying. We need to encourage people to speak out, to keep their heads up and avoid using what has become known as the 'Protestant hair shampoo' position—heads bent down with quiet voices so that no one can hear.

Fourth, it is easy to do too much talking and not enough praying. Conversational praying can be a real help. This is a time of prayer in which the praying can be 'interrupted' by a question to help the group pray further for a particular person or subject. For example, I might pray for my neighbour John because he has just lost his job. The group is not aware of this situation, so Bill asks me about it. I share a little more and Bill then goes on to pray.[2]

In whatever way we pray with others, it is important to be part of what is going on and join in with any prayer responses. One of those most commonly used is the word 'Amen', which has a Hebrew origin meaning 'I agree' or 'So be it'. It is powerful because it enables all present to join together in agreement with the prayer that has been prayed.

Whatever our hesitations, it is good to try to link up with others to pray, as it can be so encouraging. We can pray with friends over the phone, send a prayer in a letter or an email, or even text a prayer.

Praying together with others, whether in large or small groups, can have powerful results when there is common agreement and unity. In 1993, a small Friday morning prayer group was started by three men involved in full-time professional sport, and their church pastor, in the Rhondda Valley in Wales. Then, in 2001, Rhondda was named in government statistics as being the poorest part of the UK, where drug abuse and suicide claimed scores of young lives, where drug-related criminality was soaring, and where one-parent families and teen pregnancy had become the norm. The prayer group was challenged about what to do, and began to work towards a project now known as Sporting Marvels, using sport as a means of engagement to place Christian role models into local schools. Part of this initiative is the firm belief that prayer is *the* key, not a key. Delta Force 33K is an amazing vision to see each home in the 34 villages of the Rhondda prayed for on a daily basis, with the aim to raise 33,000 prayer warriors from around the world to pray blessing and joy into this place. By 2008 there were already 15,000 people from 45 countries as part of this vision, and they are seeing the impact of their prayers: in December 2007, 116 children responded to the invitation to follow Jesus at an outreach event.[3]

A prayer

Our Father, thank you that you are always with us and we are never alone. Help me to find ways to pray with and for others. Amen

Getting started

* Find an opportunity to pray with someone else or perhaps with a small group.
* If you feel hesitant about praying out loud, why not write a prayer to take with you? Alternatively choose a prayer from the Bible or a book of prayers.

* If you choose to write a prayer, remember that it could be in the form of a poem or a song. Share what you are feeling—what you want to thank God for, what you are sorry about or what you want to ask him for. Include both the positive and the negative. When you meet up with others to pray, share your prayer with them, so that they can encourage you to develop in praying aloud.

10 Prayer is a powerful weapon

Prayer is not just a relationship with God; it is also a powerful weapon, which we have been given to use wisely as we work to bring in God's kingdom. Moses is one of my prayer heroes from the Old Testament. From the time when God appeared to him in a burning bush (Exodus 3:4) right until the end of his life, he was a man who knew the power of prayer. In one example (Exodus 17), we read how he ordered Joshua to take the lead on the battlefield while he went to the top of the hill with Aaron and Hur and raised his hands in prayer over the conflict:

As long as Moses held up his hands, the Israelites were winning, but whenever he lowered his hands, the Amalekites were winning. When Moses' hands grew tired, they took a stone and put it under him and he sat on it. Aaron and Hur held his hands up—one on one side, one on the other—so that his hands remained steady till sunset. So Joshua overcame the Amalekite army with the sword (vv. 11–13).

While Joshua was fighting a physical battle, Moses engaged in spiritual combat, raising his hands in prayer over the conflict.

Prayer is the God-given means by which God's power is brought to our defence, so that we are able to stand up against the devil's schemes for ourselves and for others. We always need to remember that we have a spiritual enemy, called Satan or the devil, who was thrown out of heaven for disobeying God (Revelation 12:7–9) and was defeated by Jesus Christ on the cross (Colossians 2:15). Although he is a beaten foe, with his powers limited by God, the devil is alive and at work in our world today. It is interesting to note that Christians in Europe and North America find great difficulty in believing in the reality of evil, whereas Christians in the developing world (where the Church is growing fastest) fully appreciate the battle that is raging and use prayer as one of their weapons.

We can sometimes be unaware that Satan's main aim is to make war against Christians and prevent us from following God. Samuel Chadwick (1860–1932), a passionate Methodist preacher, said, 'The one concern of the devil is to keep us, the saints, from praying. He fears nothing from prayerless studies, prayerless work, prayerless religion. He laughs at our toil, he mocks at our wisdom, but he trembles when we pray.'

As Christians, we need to realize that we are completely hidden and safe in Christ (Colossians 3:3). Jesus has provided us with all we need to stand firm. Paul describes this in terms of a suit of armour (probably prompted by the soldiers who would have stood guard over him while he was in prison):

Stand firm then, with the belt of truth buckled around your waist, with the breastplate of righteousness in place, and with your feet fitted with the readiness that comes from the gospel of peace. In addition to all this, take up the shield of faith, with which you can extinguish all the flaming arrows of the evil one. Take the helmet of salvation and the sword of the Spirit, which is the word of God. And pray in the Spirit on all occasions with all kinds of prayers and requests (Ephesians 6:14–18).

Paul also writes, in his letter to the Christians in Rome, 'Clothe yourselves with the Lord Jesus Christ' (Romans 13:14). We need to put on, like armour, truth, righteousness, peace, faith and the salvation provided by Jesus. As a young Christian, I was given some advice that I have always found helpful—to imagine putting on the armour each morning as I got dressed, committing myself to the Lord for the day ahead.

Prayer and fasting

Fasting is also important, and this practice is mentioned many times in both Old and New Testaments. Leviticus 23:26–32 tells how God initiated fasting, and God was concerned when it was not being taken seriously by his people (Isaiah 58). We see fasting practised by individuals (Esther 4:15–16) and corporately by the Israelites (Nehemiah 9:1) in the Old Testament. Jesus taught about fasting and assumed that his followers would do it (Matthew 6:16–18). Paul fasted after his encounter with Jesus on the Damascus road (Acts 9:9), and the early Church as a whole practised fasting (Acts 13:1–3). Many church leaders down the years have believed in its importance. For example, John Wesley (who founded the movement that became the Methodist

Church) fasted every Wednesday and Friday, and gave much credit for the fruit and power of his ministry to the discipline of fasting.

Fasting enables us to humble ourselves before God, to overcome temptation, to gain understanding when seeking God's direction and to obtain God's support in order to accomplish his will. We can fast from food, from people, from the media, from the phone, from the computer and from our consumer culture in order to spend time with God in prayer.

Prayer and fasting have continued as part of the prayer culture used by Christians in many parts of the world. I remember vividly being invited, a few years ago, to one of the three days of prayer and fasting that one church network regularly hosts for its leadership teams. It was a day of worship and teaching, and we saw many answers to prayer, including a number of physical healings.

Prayer: a weapon in mission

Jesus has given us authority to go and make disciples of all nations and spread the news of his kingdom (Matthew 28:18–20). Prayer enables us to take action against the forces of darkness as they impinge on our lives and on the lives of others (2 Corinthians 10:3–5), as the following story shows. Four years before the Beachy Head Chaplaincy Team (BHCT) began, a prayer meeting had started on Beachy Head by a group of Christians praying that someone would be inspired to reach out to people who are suicidal. God answered the prayers and, since August 2004, the BHCT has been operational with the full backing of police, coastguards, social services and local churches. Prayer has continued to be a central part of the ministry and, in 2007, BHCT was involved in 670 incidents that resulted in the rescue of 248 people.

I was told about a church in America where the congregation decided to test whether it made any difference if they prayed before contacting people who lived nearby. They selected an area of 160 houses and divided them into two blocks: 80 were prayed for by the congregation and 80 were not. After a few months, the church secretary rang all 160 homes. She told them who she was and asked if they had any prayer requests, or whether they would like a visit from someone in the church. When she called the 80 homes that had not been prayed for, one person responded with a prayer request. When she called the other block, which had been prayed for, she found that 67 people responded with prayer requests and more than 40 asked for visits from the church. Prayer had opened the door for them to begin to hear about the good news, and the whole church's attitude to prayer and its role in mission changed as they realized that prayer could affect the hearts and minds of those who lived nearby.

The Message Trust, a UK based charity working in schools in inner-city Manchester and Greater Manchester, sees prayer as a central part of its mission:

Every working day in The Message offices starts with a half-hour prayer meeting. Once a week it is extended to an hour, and once a month everything stops for a whole day as everyone disappears for a prayer retreat together: performers, evangelists, administrators, technical operators, manager and directors. The whole team draws aside from the busyness of earth to refocus on the business of heaven. Message employees even have a clause in their contract that insists that they attend at least one major prayer event per month! [1]

Since it was founded, this organization, working with all its partner agencies, has seen many young people respond and follow Jesus Christ. Prayer and mission go hand in hand.

Praying for protection

The Lord's Prayer includes the phrase, 'Lead us not into temptation' (Matthew 6:13). Not only do we have our own sinful nature to contend with, but we have temptation from the secular world, and the devil wanting us to abandon prayer and discipleship altogether. We need to take our stand and pray for God's protection for ourselves and our loved ones. Celtic Christianity, which flourished in Britain from the fifth century, was characterized by a great awareness of the power of evil. Celtic Christians used special prayers of protection, called encircling prayers and breastplate prayers, in which they stated their faith in the God who was able to protect them. The most famous of these is called 'St Patrick's Breastplate', which remains a popular hymn in many churches today and can also be used as a prayer:

I bind unto myself today
The strong Name of the Trinity,

By invocation of the same,
The Three in One and One in Three.

We can be prompted to pray for protection in the most surprising ways. A friend and I arrived in Bradford the evening before we were due to go as part of the prayer team for the annual Maundy Thursday service in the cathedral, at which the Queen, accompanied by Prince Philip, hands out Maundy money. Our hotel had provided a kettle in the bedroom and we immediately put it on for a welcome cup of tea, but it did not work. Eventually we had to take it to the manager, who told us the fuse was faulty. I was unexpectedly called away, but my friend spent time praying. When I returned, she told me that the Lord had reminded her of the fuse on the kettle and she had found herself praying for protection for the cathedral. A few days later, we discovered that at the exact time she was praying, a device with fuses had been discovered in the cathedral and disposed of safely.

On another occasion, I found myself needing special protection when I had to pray for a burglar to be caught. The flat where I was living in central Oxford had been robbed two days running, in spite of the fact that we had changed the locks. As the police were getting worried, they decided to leave an officer in the hallway on duty during the night. I resolved, together with friends who lived downstairs, that we would pray for the burglar to return to the house. We told the officer and started to pray, with my other flatmate keeping a watch upstairs. As we prayed, the man approached the back door, which we had left closed but unlocked. As the burglar began to open the door, I shall never forget the policeman greeting him with the standard phrase, 'Good evening, sir, you are under arrest!' After a fight in the hall, he was taken away and we were safe again.

We do well to meditate on these words of Karl Barth, a Swiss theologian (1886–1968), who said, 'To clasp hands in prayer is the beginning of an uprising against the disorder of the world.'

A prayer

Mighty God, thank you for providing all I need to withstand the enemy. Help me to stand firm and trust you for your help and victory. Amen

Getting started

* Use a passage of scripture to pray for someone you are concerned about—for example, Psalm 34 in relation to somebody struggling with fear. This can be done on your own or with others in a small group. Start by reading verses 1–3 and, recalling how God has helped you, turn that recollection into prayers of praise and thanksgiving. Then look at verses 4 and 6 and pray for the person on your mind. Finally look at verse 5 with the promise that it carries, and use that verse as an inspiration for prayer.[2]

* Use worship and fasting together. Read Ephesians 6:14–18. Find space to be with God on your own; you may want to fast from food for one meal to give him your undivided attention. Come humbly, just as

you are, and give him the concerns you are carrying. Listen to some praise and worship music (of whatever style you like). Soak in what you are hearing and start to worship, bringing into your worship the person or situation that you are concerned about. Ask God for his strength to be shown and his power to change whatever needs to be changed—in yourself or in any others for whom you are praying. Continue to praise and pray, responding to the Holy Spirit's leading. This type of praise praying can be used time and time again and helps to strengthen and encourage us for the battles we face.

11 Prayer: when, where, how?

When should I pray?

We can pray at any time. Prayer was part of Jesus' daily routine. He prayed early in the morning (Luke 4:42), he frequently withdrew to pray (5:16) and he sometimes prayed all night (6:12).

We can pray at the same time each day and we can pray at odd moments during the day. What is important is to make space to meet with God each day. I have heard it said that the difference between catching a few moments with the Lord and having quality time with him is like the difference between driving through a fast-food restaurant and spending the evening at a restaurant with a good friend. At the takeaway you drive up, give your order, drive to the window and eat in the car. In the restaurant, you sit down, spend time in conversation, enjoy the food in a leisurely way and leave satisfied and nourished.

If we don't have a regular time to enjoy the company of God, we are the ones who miss out. Jesus found that his best time to talk with his Father was early in the morning, and that is what works for me, too. It will not be the best time for everyone, but our challenge is to find out what works for us and make room for God in our busy lifestyles. It can be helpful to ask ourselves questions such as 'When do I find it easiest to pray?' or 'When do I find it hardest to pray?'

Where can I pray?

Jesus talked about the importance of finding a special place where we won't be distracted (Matthew 6:6), which is as much about finding inner space to tune into God as it is about finding a specific physical place. A 17th-century monk, Brother Lawrence, developed his own way of 'practising the presence of God'. As he worked in the monastery kitchen, he learned to experience the reality of God's presence by getting into the habit of turning his heart and mind towards God throughout the day.[1] This discipline of remembering God's presence is particularly important for our fast-paced 21st-century lifestyles.

Some people love to spend time with God in the same place each day, but that does not necessarily work for others. I am often travelling to work at a different time and to a different location each day. I have learnt that I can pray anywhere, as I travel or wait in a queue, at my workplace, in the kitchen, in the garden or out on a long country walk.

How long should I pray for?

This really is up to you. You may have three minutes, five minutes, 15 minutes or an hour; what is important is that you begin with a period of time that you know you can manage. God isn't necessarily looking for a long session every time we start to pray, but he is looking for a heart turned towards him. Sometimes it may be just five minutes but there will be other times when, as we stop and draw near, God draws near too, and there is such closeness of fellowship that the time just slips away.

Short prayers can be very useful. I think my most often-used prayer is 'Help, Lord!' This type of praying is often called 'arrow praying'. In Nehemiah 2, we read of the conversation between Nehemiah and King Arta-xerxes. Nehemiah had just heard about the ruined state of the city of Jerusalem and God had laid it on his heart that he was to help with the rebuilding. When the king asked Nehemiah, 'What is it you want?' we read, 'Then I prayed to the God of heaven, and I answered the king' (vv. 4–5). There was no time for a long prayer, only something short and to the point.

How do I pray?

As we have seen, prayer is as simple as picking up the telephone and talking. You can start where you want and say what you want. Some people find it helpful to use a simple framework, such as the ACTS model (Adoration, Confession, Thanksgiving and Supplication), as a start-ing point. Working through each type of prayer, you can spend a few moments on each for yourself and for others, asking the Holy Spirit to lead and guide.

Another idea is to work through the Lord's Prayer, using each phrase as a prompt to pray for yourself and others.[2] Yet another is to use the Anglican daily office of morning and evening prayer, which can be very helpful if you like to follow a liturgical framework.[3]

Once I begin to pray, I usually find that there are lots of people or issues that I could pray for, so I find it helpful to divide up my times of prayer and tune in to God at various points through the day. A friend of mine uses her daily walk with her dog to pray for particular people she knows at certain parts of her route.

How do I handle distractions?

As we start to pray, we all face the problem of distractions. Because of the busy lifestyles we lead, the moment we stop, our minds fill with everything else but God. In saying that, though, not all of what we call 'distractions' are in fact such, and I have begun to realize that it is only when I stop and allow the thoughts to roll around my mind that I can get clarity on something that has eluded me thus far.

Here are a few hints I have picked up over the years:

- If you are distracted by thinking about jobs you need to do, keep a pen and paper handy, jot them down as you think about them and then return to seeking God in prayer.
- If you are suddenly reminded of a person or situation, which keeps coming back to mind, include it in your prayer time.
- If the phone keeps ringing, ignore it, unplug it or use an answerphone—but remember to check who called afterwards.
- If you are bombarded with thoughts or images that draw you away from God's values and character, ask him to remove them from your mind.
- A passage of scripture can be a good place to come back to if your thoughts have wandered, as you can return to the passage you had been reading before.

How can I remember what to pray for?

There are a number of ways to keep track of our prayers, and we can choose whatever seems most appropriate for us.

- A prayer journal can be helpful, to write down Bible verses, key points about our times of prayer, favourite prayers by other people and our own prayers to God.
- A prayer diary is useful for recording what we pray for others and how we receive answers. I remember a time when a number of us in a home group kept such a diary at our weekly early-morning prayer meeting. We were amazed when we started to see just how much God did answer our prayers.
- Prayer lists are good—if you like lists! You can have a daily, weekly or monthly list, choosing two or three people or issues for each day.
- A photoboard is excellent, especially when praying with children and for those we don't see on a regular basis.

Do I have to pray aloud?

Praying out loud is no more important than praying silently, but it helps if you want others to pray with you and be able to agree with your prayers. I remember the first time I prayed out loud, at a study group for new Christians. The person leading that evening had taught us about prayer and then suggested that it would be good if we all prayed out loud one after another, and so we went around the circle. By the time it was my turn,

I could feel my heart pounding and I didn't know if I would be able to do it. But we had been given some very helpful advice, which was to thank God for our favourite verse from the chapter of the Bible we had just been reading. So I found my favourite verse and remember saying in a very quiet voice, 'Thank you, Lord, for verse such-and-such.' I felt such a relief as the sound barrier had been broken, and from then on we had no problems praying as a group. I have enjoyed praying out loud ever since, and helping others to do the same.

If you want to start to pray out loud, you could write out your prayers and get used to hearing your own voice when you are on your own. Another way is to read a verse of scripture and then pray it back to God aloud. For example, take Matthew 6:34: 'Therefore do not worry about tomorrow, for tomorrow will worry about itself. Each day has enough trouble of its own.' After reading this, you could pray, 'Thank you, Lord, that you have promised that I do not need to worry. Please help me not to worry about… [list whatever you are worried about] and help me to trust you for today.'

Should I sit, kneel or stand?

It does not matter to God whether we stand, kneel, sit, walk or lie face down on the floor. We can do whatever feels most natural for us. When I am on my own, I find I want to sit sometimes, kneel sometimes, and go for a walk on other occasions.

Through the Bible we see examples of how different postures for prayer are used. We see David dancing before the Lord (2 Samuel 6:14) and Elisha lying on top of the dead Shunammite boy, praying for life to return (2 Kings 4:32–34). We can stand before the majesty of God (1 Kings 19:11); we can lift up our arms (Psalm 141.2; 1 Timothy 2:8); we can lift our eyes (Psalm 123:1–2); we can kneel (1 Kings 8:54) or prostrate ourselves (2 Chronicles 20:18). As we worship and adore God, we may want to lift our heads (and hands) upwards. As we spend time in saying sorry, it may be more appropriate to kneel, lie on the floor or bow our heads. And we can use our hands in this way:

- Start with clenched fists. As we praise and confess to God, we can open our hands as we receive his love and cleansing.
- Cup our hands (as if holding something in them) as we silently give thanks for all we have received from God during the day. Then we can reach out with our hands (as if showing God the needs of the people on our heart or his suffering world) and pray for those who are in any kind of pain.
- Finally, we can lift up our hands (as if to welcome) and express our trust and hope in God.

What is important is that each of us offers our whole self to God when we come to prayer, as Paul writes: 'Therefore, I urge you, brothers and sisters, in view of God's mercy, to offer your bodies as living sacrifices, holy and pleasing to God—this is your spiritual act of worship' (Romans 12:1).

A prayer

Lord Jesus, I still have many questions about prayer but I want to make a start. Please show me good times for me to pray and help me to get going. Amen

Getting started

* Try praying through the Lord's Prayer.
* 'Our Father in heaven, hallowed be your Name': Use this time to worship and thank him for who he is and what he has done.
* 'Your kingdom come, your will be done on earth as it is in heaven': Use this phrase to prompt prayers for your loved ones, situations at work, your church and nation, and be led by the Holy Spirit to pray about issues around the world.
* 'Give us this day our daily bread': What needs do you have today, practically and spiritually? What are the needs of your loved ones, neighbours, colleagues and so on?
* 'And forgive us our sins as we forgive those who sin against us': Use this phrase for internal reflection about receiving forgiveness from God and releasing forgiveness to others.
* 'And lead us not into temptation but deliver us from evil': Use this phrase to allow yourself to surrender again to the love of Jesus, knowing that as you take refuge in him and ask for his help, he will enable you to stand firm.

* 'For yours is the kingdom, the power and the glory, for ever': End with praise and worship.

12 Prayer is not always easy

Prayer is a huge subject and we have only touched the very tip of it in this book. Before we finish, though, we need to look at one more important area: coping with difficulties in prayer. It would be wrong to give the impression that prayer is always easy or that all prayers get answered quickly. Prayer is not necessarily going to be easy and it is not something that we can do simply when the mood takes us. It will often be hard work and a real struggle, but we are called to persevere (Luke 18:1–8), for prayer is one of the most important tasks that God has given to his children.

Most of us, if we are honest, will admit that we find prayer difficult. I know I do. It demands time, which we never seem to have. It requires concentration when our thoughts are on other matters. It calls for endless patience. How do we cope? Here are some helpful tips that I have learnt.

First, we need to make prayer part of our lives—indeed, a daily habit—if we want to learn to pray. Experts tell us that it takes the average person 30 days of doing the same thing before it becomes a habit. We need to become disciplined about prayer and make a habit of meeting with God. I know people who put in their diary a lunch-hour with God each week, or extended time at weekends if it is not possible during the week.

Second, we need to remember, in the words of the Catholic priest and scholar John Chapman, to 'pray as you can, and not as you cannot'. I meet so many people who feel guilty about what they are not doing when it comes to prayer that they never get started. God certainly doesn't want us to remain like that. We need to confess our failure but then we should start to pray for as long as we can manage, asking God by his Spirit to lead and guide us. And remember: just wanting to pray is prayer; a sigh is prayer; tears can be prayer; for God knows what is on our hearts.

Third, we need to understand that our timing is not the same as God's timing, and we have to learn to wait for God—something that I often find difficult. Fortunately, I have a wise friend who often reminds me that 'God is never in a hurry as his timing is always perfect'. While God does answer our prayers, he may not necessarily do so in the way that we want, because he sees the bigger picture and he knows how it all fits together. Looking at the wrong side of a half-finished piece of tapestry, it is hard to imagine that there is a picture in the making. Threads are hanging, waiting to be linked up again, and colours seem to run everywhere. But when we turn it over and look at the right side, we can see how each thread works to make up the picture, often having to wait its turn before being woven in. It is much the same with our prayers. They each have their turn to be slotted in to make God's picture complete.

Fourth, we need to remember that sin can be a barrier, preventing our prayers from being heard by God. He is not able to answer our prayers if we know of unconfessed sin in our hearts (see Isaiah 59:2), if we are disobedient to what he may have asked us to do (1 John 3:21–22), if we have wrong motives in our asking (James 4:2–3), or if we haven't bothered to find out his will in a given situation.

Does God answer all our prayers?

This is a huge question, which cannot be dealt with in detail in this book, but here are some insights.

God may answer with a 'Yes—I thought you'd never ask'. These replies usually come very quickly. He may answer with a 'Yes—but not yet', which can be much more difficult to handle. This is the time when we need to hold on to God and not let go, even though we can't understand what's happening. When I first became a Christian, I found that I received answers much more quickly and more obviously than I do now. I think that has to do with the fact that I did not have any experience of how to live a life following God, so he needed to step in quickly to keep me going. As I have gone on in my walk with him, I have found that he expects me to learn, remember and obey all that he has taught me over the years.

God may answer 'Yes—but not in the way you think'. One month before the elections in South Africa in 1994, a policeman was praying about the situation when he had a vision of an angel, who told him, 'I want South Africa on its knees in prayer. You have 14 days to go to the highest authority.' The policeman was astonished but did as he was told. He went to President F.W. de Klerk, who agreed, and 6 April—Founders' Day—was declared a day of prayer for South Africa. Many believe that this prayer, linked to all the other prayer and reconciliation that had taken place behind the scenes, made it possible for the final agreement to be reached, ending apartheid.[1] I don't for one moment think that the policeman expected to be involved in that way. We have to be willing to be part of the answer to our own prayers.

God may answer with a 'No—I love you too much'. These are the answers that we discover only when we look back on a situation. Sometimes we ask for things that are just not right for us, like a three-year-old asking their parents for an electric drill for Christmas. I remember hearing the late Ruth Graham (wife of evangelist Billy Graham) recounting the story of how she prayed and prayed that the man she was going out with at the time would ask her to marry him. In later years, she was so grateful to God that he had answered her prayer with a 'No', for at that time she had not yet met Billy and she subsequently realized what a disaster the other marriage would have been.

God may also answer with what appears to be a straight 'No'. This is very hard to handle, especially if we are praying for a loved one who is sick, for a member of our family to find faith in Christ, or for someone suffering from an addiction. A good friend of mine died earlier this year, having been diagnosed with a terminal disease three years previously. We had joined him and his family in praying for him, and saw a wonderful healing which amazed even the doctors—but then the illness returned. We know he is now in a better place, but that doesn't make the situation any easier. Fiona Castle, speaking after the death of her husband Roy in 1994, said:

I would never underestimate the value of prayer. I really believe that although perhaps prayer was not answered in the way we would have liked to see it answered, I honestly believe that through the prayers of the faithful people who prayed for Roy… he was strong, he was faithful to the end. I believe that through prayer we were given opportunities to share our faith.

We should always remember that there is so much more to healing than physical healing, and to be with God, where there is no more crying and no more pain (Revelation 21:4), is, for many people, the best healing there could ever be.

Some prayers seem to go unanswered as far as we can see from our perspective. Philip Yancey lists some biblical examples: for instance, King David prayed for his son not to die, but he did; Moses, Job, Jonah and Elijah prayed to die, but they didn't; Paul prayed three times for his 'thorn in the flesh' to be removed, but it wasn't.[2] Pete Greig (the founder of the 24–7 Prayer movement) handles this issue of unanswered prayer as he writes from the pain of his wife's fight for life:

Some prayers aren't answered because God Himself is a greater Answer than the thing we are asking for, and He wants to use our sense of need to draw us into a deeper relationship with Himself.

Pete goes on to say:

There is something solemn I must tell you (and this may well have been the hardest line to write in the whole book):

I have come to believe that if Samie had been spared her brain tumour and we'd never been forced to face the possibility of her early death, we would thereby have missed out on God's best for our lives.[3]

Whatever the situation we are facing, I have learnt that it is best to be really honest with God about whatever is happening. I am so glad that the story about Hannah is in the Bible (1 Samuel 1:1–20). God does not appear to Hannah at all; he does not speak or give her promises, but out of her deep relationship with him, Israel's future is secured. Hannah was in a difficult situation, because God had not answered her prayers and she was barren, while her husband's other wife had children. Her husband loved her very much, but that was just not enough. Hannah couldn't stand it any more, so she cried to God in silence from her innermost longings, 'in bitterness of soul' (v. 10). As Hannah poured out her heart, Eli the priest was watching and thought she was drunk. But when she explained her difficulty, he immediately recognized that God was with this woman and blessed her. Hannah's story ended happily as she did have a son. Amazingly, because of her gratitude, she gave him back to God and he became a mighty leader in Israel. We need to learn to be truly honest before God, because he is big enough to cope with all our disappointments, anger and frustrations.

Learning to trust when God seems far away

Most of us will experience a time in our lives when it feels as if God has gone on a long walk and left us far behind. It can take many forms and can last for a few days, weeks, months or even longer. We may find Bible reading dull, our prayers feel as if they are hitting the ceiling, and we may experience doubts about our faith.

Sometimes there are reasons for this experience, such as unconfessed sin in our lives, but more often it is simply God's way of teaching us to depend on him more and more. That was the case for me after starting a new job in Canada, when I experienced a long time when God seemed far away. I survived by sharing my situation with a couple of very close friends, by continuing to read my Bible each day, by still attending church and using books of prayers to keep in touch with God when my own words dried up. God did eventually appear back on the scene—and when he did, I found that I had learnt so much more about living from a place of complete trust, even though I couldn't understand what I was going through at the time.

Learning from others

It can also be very helpful to find out more about prayer from our friends, from people in our church or from our own reading. We can study prayers in the Bible: for example, Moses talking with the Lord (Exodus 33:12–18), Daniel praying for his nation (Daniel 9:4–19), Jesus praying for his disciples (John 17:6–26), or Paul praying for a church (Colossians 1:3–8; Ephesians 3:14–19).

We can learn from websites, which provide a variety of options. For example, www.sacredspace.ie offers a daily meditation based on scripture passages. You can download daily prayers on to MP3 players and computers from www.pray-as-you-go.org. Each of the denominations has resources to help and encourage personal prayer. You can read some of the books and check out some of the websites that I have mentioned throughout this book.

I end with a quotation from Henri Nouwen, which I have often found helpful:

Once, quite a few years ago, I had the opportunity of meeting Mother Teresa of Calcutta. I was struggling with many things at the time and decided to use the occasion to ask Mother Teresa's advice. As soon as we sat down I started explaining all my problems and difficulties—trying to convince her of how complicated it all was! When, after ten minutes of elaborate explanation, I finally became silent, Mother Teresa looked at me quietly and said: 'Well, when you spend one hour a day adoring your Lord and never do anything which you know is wrong... you will be fine!' ... In fact I was so stunned by her answer that I didn't feel any desire or need to continue the conversation... I knew she had spoken the truth and that I had the rest of my life to live it… I realize that I had raised a question from below and she had given an answer from above.[4]

We will always have struggles with prayer because we will never fully understand who God is and how he works. But let's remember to be honest with God and with ourselves and pour out our hearts to him, trusting in his love, his promises and his mercy to hear our prayers, remembering that he will never leave us or forsake us (Matthew 28:20).

A prayer

Loving Lord, yes, I have found prayer difficult and sometimes have not known how to begin. Please help me not to be put off by what I can't do. I do want to follow you, love you and trust you more. Amen

Notes

Introduction

1 www.prayerforum.org
2 Patrick Johnstone and Jason Mandryk, *Operation World* (Authentic Lifestyle, 2001)
3 www.gatewaymedia.org.uk

Chapter 2

1 Tom Wright, *A Moment of Prayer* (Lion, 1995)
2 Richard Foster, *Prayer: Finding the Heart's True Home* (Hodder & Stoughton, 1992)
3 Clement of Alexandria (c.150–215)
4 John Henry Newman (1801–90)
5 Wright, *A Moment of Prayer*

Chapter 3

1 www.worthabbey.net
2 www.retreats.org.uk
3 www.tearfund.org (Search for 'Prayer in the UK')
4 John Humphys, *In God We Doubt* (Hodder & Stoughton, 2007)
5 Jonathan Aitken, *Psalms for People under Pressure* (The Athlone Press, 2004)
6 For a fuller explanation of this, see Andy Flannagan, *God 360: 120 Experiential Devotions* (Authentic Media, 2006)

Chapter 4

1 Westminster Shorter Catechism (1674)
2 www.taize.fr
3 www.ihop.org
4 www.prodigals.org.uk; Rob Parsons, *Bringing Home the Prodigals* (Hodder & Stoughton, 2003)
5 There are about 350 different names for God as Father, Son and Holy Spirit in the article 'Pray in Jesus's Name' on www.ipcprayer.org/resources.asp
6 Global Day of Prayer UK: www.globaldayofprayer.co.uk; worldwide: www.globaldayofprayer.com
7 Graham Cooke, *Beholding and Becoming* (Sovereign World, 2004)

Chapter 5

1 For example, Angel Ashwin, *Book of a Thousand Prayers* (Zondervan, 2002)
2 C.S. Lewis, 'On forgiveness', in *The Weight of Glory* (Zondervan, 2001)
3 http://news.bbc.co.uk/1/hi/england/ merseyside/4471440.stm
4 *Joy Magazine* (New Life Publishing, May 2008)
5 Debra Green, *Redeeming Our Communities* (New Wine, 2008)
6 Foster, *Prayer*

Chapter 7

1 David Barker, pastor and part of the Churches
   Together Schools Team Kent, *Prayer Magazine*,
   April–June 2008 (New Life Publishing)
2 Redeeming our Communities:
   www.redeemingourcommunities.org.uk;
   Street Pastors: www.streetpastors.org.uk;
   Adopt a Cop: www.cpauk.net
3 Debra Green, *Redeeming our Communities*, which
   contains many stories of answers to prayer

Chapter 8

1 Abbot Christopher Jamison, *Finding Sanctuary*
   (Phoenix, 2007)
2 *Woman and Home*, April 2008, p. 17
3 D. Foster, *Reading with God: Lectio Divina*
   (Continuum Publishing, 2005); Richard Foster,
   Life with God (Hodder & Stoughton, 2008)
4 Quiet Garden: www.quietgarden.co.uk;
   Contemplative Fire: www.contemplativefire.org
5 Suggestions taken from Margaret Silf, *Taste and See*
   (DLT, 1999)
6 Community Watchmen Ministries:
   www.cwmprayer.com

Chapter 9

1 Celia Bowring, 'Teach ourselves to pray for schools', *Prayer Magazine*, April–June 2008: www.prayermagazine.net; Schools Prayer Network: www.schoolsprayernetwork.org.uk

2 See Jane Holloway, *Community Prayer Cells: How to Be Good News Neighbours* (CPAS, 1998)

3 www.sportingmarvels.com

Chapter 10

1 Frank and Debra Green, *City-Changing Prayer* (Survivor, 2005)

2 See Fresh Prayer resources on www.waymakers.org

Chapter 11

1 Brother Lawrence, *The Practice of the Presence of God* (Baker, 1999)

2 Tom Wright, *The Lord and His Prayer* (Triangle, 1996)

3 *Common Worship: Daily Prayers* (www.cofe.anglican.org)

Chapter 12

1 Michael Cassidy, *A Witness Forever* (Hodder & Stoughton, 1995)

2 Philip Yancey, *Prayer: Does It Make Any Difference?* (Hodder & Stoughton, 2006)

3 Pete Greig, *God on Mute* (Survivor, 2007)

4 Henri Nouwen, *Here and Now: Living in the Spirit* (DLT, 1994)

Also from BRF

Bible Reading—a Beginner's Guide

Michael Green

The Bible may be the bestselling book in the world, but reading it—let alone understanding and applying it to daily life—can be a daunting prospect even for people who feel they are some way along the road of Christian discipleship. Where do we start? How do we work out its relevance to us? If we feel we know it quite well already, how can we go further in exploring its riches?

This highly accessible book sets out straightforward and helpful strategies for those who are completely new to Bible reading, which can also benefit those who have begun to develop a Bible-reading habit and want to broaden and deepen their understanding. Step by step, Michael Green explains how to enjoy the Bible (and avoid feeling bored by it!), how to read it by ourselves and benefit from discussing it with others, and how we in turn can start to share its teaching with new Christians.

ISBN 978 1 84101 610 8   £4.99

Available from your local Christian bookshop or, in case of difficulty, direct from BRF using the order form on page 109.

ORDER FORM

REF	TITLE	PRICE	QTY	TOTAL
610 8	Bible Reading—a Beginner's Guide	£4.99		

POSTAGE AND PACKING CHARGES				
Order value	UK	Europe	Surface	Air Mail
£7.00 & under	£1.25	£3.00	£3.50	£5.50
£7.10–£30.00	£2.25	£5.50	£6.50	£10.00
Over £30.00	FREE	prices on request		

Postage and packing	
Donation	
TOTAL	

Name _____ Account Number _____

Address _____

_____ Postcode _____

Telephone Number_____

Email _____

Payment by: ❏ Cheque ❏ Mastercard ❏ Visa ❏ Postal Order ❏ Maestro

Card no ⬛⬛⬛⬛ ⬛⬛⬛⬛ ⬛⬛⬛⬛ ⬛⬛⬛⬛ ⬛⬛

Valid from ⬛⬛⬛⬛   Expires ⬛⬛⬛⬛   Issue no. ⬛⬛⬛

Security code* ⬛⬛⬛   *Last 3 digits on the reverse of the card.   Shaded boxes for
ESSENTIAL IN ORDER TO PROCESS YOUR ORDER   Maestro use only

Signature _____ Date _____

All orders must be accompanied by the appropriate payment.

Please send your completed order form to:
BRF, 15 The Chambers, Vineyard, Abingdon OX14 3FE
Tel. 01865 319700 / Fax. 01865 319701 Email: enquiries@brf.org.uk

❏ Please send me further information about BRF publications.

Available from your local Christian bookshop.   BRF is a Registered Charity

brf

Resourcing your spiritual journey

through...

- Bible reading notes
- Books for Advent & Lent
- Books for Bible study and prayer
- Books to resource those working with
  under 11s in school, church and at home

- Quiet days and retreats
- Training for primary teachers
  and children's leaders
- Godly Play
- Barnabas RE Days

For more information, visit the **brf** website
at **www.brf.org.uk**